BLUEBELL RAILWAY
LOCOMOTIVES

AS THEY WERE

Robert Inns and John Scott-Morgan

Midland Publishing Limited

Bluebell Railway Locomotives - As they Were
© 1996 Robert Inns and John Scott-Morgan
ISBN 1 85780 036 2

First published in 1996 by
Midland Publishing Limited
24 The Hollow, Earl Shilton
Leicester, LE9 7NA, England
Tel: 01455 847815 Fax: 01455 841805

Design concept and layout
© 1996 Midland Publishing Limited and
Stephen Thompson Associates

Printed in England by
Clearpoint Colourprint Limited
Daybrook, Nottingham, NG5 6HD

This book is dedicated to Mary, Robert's wife,
for her encouragement and support and to all
members of the Bluebell Railway Preservation
Society, both past and present.

Front cover: **In August 1962 No 75027 pilots
rebuilt Bulleid 'West Country' Pacific No
34040 *Crewkerne* on a Manchester to
Bournemouth train, at Midford on the
Somerset & Dorset line.** W Potter / Colour-Rail

Back cover, top: **BR Standard class 5 No 73082
Camelot hurries a down parcels working
through Micheldever in May 1962.** Colour-Rail

Back cover, bottom: **A very clean 'USA' tank
No 30064 is seen on shed at Guildford on
13th October 1964.** Colour-Rail

Title page: **No 33001, the only survivor of
Bulleid's wartime-built Q1 class 0-6-0s, now
part of the National Railway Museum's
collection and on long term loan to the
Bluebell Railway, leaves Bramley & Wonersh
station in 1961.** Mike Esau

This page: **BR Standard class 4 4-6-0
No 75027, pilots an unidentified 9F 2-10-0
through Wellow on the former Somerset &
Dorset line with the northbound 'The Pines
Express' on 4th August 1962.** J G Dewing

Facing page: **'Schools' class No 928 *Stowe*
shunting at Clapham Junction on
24th March 1935.** H F Wheeler collection,
courtesy R S Carpenter

Preface and Acknowledgements

The locomotives of the Bluebell Railway are as varied and as interesting a collection of machines as can be found anywhere in Britain today.

The photographic record of these engines during their careers, before they were saved for preservation, varies enormously. Some of the older locomotives like the 'Terriers' and our particular Bluebell favourite, the Adams Radial Tank, were very well recorded throughout their long lives. Perhaps surprisingly, the group of locomotives which probably gave us the most difficulty when it came to tracking down good quality pictures, was the British Railways Standard classes, in particular No 78059, which nearly drove us both to despair.

One particular problem which presented itself early in the course of our work on this project, was the simple one of the best sequence in which to deal with the Bluebell locomotives. Having looked at the various options, in the end we decided to present the engines in order of the numbers which they carried when withdrawn by British Railways, with the industrial locomotives bringing up the rear. This has led to a largely SR book being headed by a GWR locomotive, albeit a unique one, and also means that some of the engines are listed here under numbers which they have not normally carried in their service on the Bluebell Railway, the Adams tank No 488 being a case in point.

We would like to express our appreciation and thanks to all those who have helped us during the preparation of this book, in particular to the photographers and keepers of photographic collections who have supplied material. Our special gratitude goes to Tom Middlemass, R M Casserley, R C Stumpf, G T V Stacey, Mike Gilchrist, Ray Stephens and Mike Esau.

The information in this book has been obtained from a variety of magazines, periodicals and books too numerous to list. In this connection we have used material held at The Railway Club, London; the National Railway Museum, York; and the Public Records Office, Kew, and offer our grateful thanks to the curators and staff of the latter two organisations.

Thanks are due to the team at Midland Publishing, especially Russell, Steve and Chris for shaping the book you have in your hands. Our thanks are also due to John Fry and Laurie Bowles for taking the trouble to read the proofs and drawing our attention to various anomalies which had crept into the text and captions.

These glimpses of the working lives of the locomotives which have found sanctuary on the Bluebell Railway will, we hope, inform and be of interest to all those who share our affection for that most magnificent of machines, the steam locomotive.

We have very much enjoyed researching and writing this book and would like to think that it may add, in some small way, to a greater appreciation of the magnificent achievements of the Bluebell Railway and the various locomotive-owning groups based on it, in keeping the sight and sounds of the steam locomotive alive in the heart of southern England.

Robert Inns and John Scott-Morgan
April 1996

Introduction

What is today the Bluebell Railway was promoted by the Lewes & East Grinstead Railway Company, which was formed in 1876, to link the towns in its title. The L&EG was backed by the London Brighton & South Coast Railway, ever anxious to protect its territory from possible incursions by its great rival, the South Eastern. The line was opened on 1st August 1882 and shortly afterwards the nominally independent L&EG was absorbed by the LB&SCR. On 3rd September 1883 a branch from Haywards Heath, on the main London to Brighton line, to Horsted Keynes on the erstwhile L&EG, was opened.

Double track was laid between East Grinstead and Horsted Keynes and on the branch to Haywards Heath. South of Horsted Keynes the formation allowed for a double line but only one track was laid. The line never amounted to more than a rural byway and as such it prospered in the years up to the Great War. Like so many rural lines in Britain it began to lose traffic to the roads from the 1920s onwards. In 1923 the LB&SCR, along with the other railways in the south of England, became part of the Southern Railway.

The SR had ambitious plans to electrify much of its network between the wars. Among the lines to be electrified in 1935 was the section from Haywards Heath to Horsted Keynes, the first part of a bigger scheme to extend the third rail from Croydon through East Grinstead to Lewes. The outbreak of hostilities in 1939 put a stop to these plans which were never revived after the war thus leaving the rural Horsted Keynes the unlikely terminus of what was a short electrified branch line from Haywards Heath.

Despite various economies, by the mid-1950s the line from Lewes to Horsted Keynes was clearly losing money and British Railways proposed its closure, the last service train running on 28th May 1955. However, in an episode that would have been worthy of an Ealing comedy, that was not the end of the story. A local resident, a Miss Bessemer, discovered that the British Transport Commission had no right to close the line as the original L&EG Act of Parliament, which was still in force, had stipulated that a service of four trains each day stopping at stations specified in the Act, had to

be operated. BR had no option but to resume this basic service to these stations, which it did in August 1956, until amending legislation could be enacted. BR behaved with singularly bad grace in relation to these 'parliamentary' trains which were run at inconvenient times and sailed through those stations not mentioned in the original Act, without stopping.

Parliamentary approval for the closure plans was eventually obtained and the final trains ran for the second and now definitely the last time, on 16th March 1958. The stay of execution provided by the intervention of Miss Bessemer had however brought the line fame far beyond Sussex. Known popularly as the Bluebell Line because of the profusion of these flowers which could be seen along its route in Spring, a meeting was held in Haywards Heath on 14th June 1959 which led to the formation of the Bluebell Railway Preservation Society. The section of line from Sheffield Park to just south of Horsted Keynes became, from 7th August 1960, the first standard gauge branch line in Britain, to be operated by preservationists.

Adams Radial tank No 30583, ex-works at Eastleigh in 1959, having received an Adams pattern boiler in the course of an overhaul completed in March of that year.
Philip J Kelley

It is salutary to reflect that the first trains ran on the Bluebell in the same year as British Railways built its last steam locomotive. The fact that it was a pioneer of standard gauge preservation was to give the Bluebell in time a fleet of steam locomotives of remarkable character. Its existence also provided a stimulus to groups and individuals who now had somewhere to place locomotives which they were contemplating preserving. Among the acquisitions in the early years were a pair of LB&SCR 'Terriers' as well as two of their South Eastern & Chatham equivalents, the P class 0-6-0 tanks. The only surviving examples of the L&SWR Adams 4-4-2T and the Brighton E4 class 0-6-2T were also early arrivals on the Bluebell.

In later years the unfortunate demise of other preservation schemes such as those based at the former steam shed at Ashford and on the Longmoor Military Railway brought more unique locomotives to the Bluebell such as the only survivors of the SE&CR C and H classes and the line's first Bulleid Pacific, No 34023 *Blackmore Vale*. When in the 1970s the eyes of railway enthusiasts turned to Woodham's scrapyard in Barry as a source of additional locomotives, those which found homes on the Bluebell were machines which had associations with the railways of the south of England in one form or another, such as examples of the Brighton built Standard class 4 tanks, which worked on the Bluebell in BR days or No 73082 *Camelot*, one of the Standard 4-6-0 class 5s allocated to the Southern Region which took the names of withdrawn SR 'King Arthurs'.

The visitor to the Bluebell Railway will enjoy a locomotive fleet which offers both variety and coherence and in a number of cases, where the Bluebell example is the only one of its type to survive, uniqueness, which few railways in Britain can rival. There are no lines of ex-BR diesels here to intrude on this paradise for SR steam enthusiasts. In the pages that follow, as we explore aspects of the pre-preservation careers of the locomotives which now make up the Bluebell fleet, it is gratifying to realise just what a wealth of fascinating machines have been preserved rather than be saddened by thoughts of some which should have escaped the clutches of the scrapman, but did not.

Miss Bessemer, the founding fathers of the Society and the many groups and individuals who have worked hard over the years to preserve and restore so many fine machines, are all worthy of our grateful thanks. When the Bluebell achieves its long term ambition and the line is extended to East Grinstead where a link with the national network will once again be established, it is reassuring to know that the railway will have the capacity in its locomotive fleet to cover both the increased mileages and, hopefully, the greater numbers of passengers which the fully rebuilt northern extension will generate.

'USA' tanks, No 30064 in the foreground, and No 30072, are seen at Southampton Docks on 17th July 1961. Both of these locomotives have been preserved, No 30064 is on the Bluebell and No 30072 can be seen on the Keighley & Worth Valley Railway.
Colin Hogg, courtesy Mike Esau

No 9017

From early in its history the Great Western Railway operated a policy of standardisation, having parts interchangeable between different types of locomotives. During the 1930s many new locomotives were being constructed using parts from withdrawn engines; for instance, the 'Grange' and 'Manor' 4-6-0s were built using wheels and motion from withdrawn 43xx 2-6-0s.

The Great Western Railway built the 3252 'Duke' class between 1895 and 1899, 60 being constructed, and the 33xx 'Bulldog' class from 1899 to 1910. In this period 136 'Bulldogs' were built. Between 1902 and 1909 twenty 3252 class locomotives were reboilered with the standard No 2 boilers used on the 'Bulldogs'.

In the 1930s the reverse of this process took place. The frames of withdrawn 33xx class engines were fitted with small N class boilers from 3252 class locomotives to create the new 32xx 'Earl' class. The prototype was No 3265 *Tre Pol and Pen*, constructed in 1929. The GWR then issued Lot numbers for 40 rebuilds, to be numbered 3200 to 3239, inclusive. However only the locomotives up to and including No 3228 had been completed by the outbreak of the Second World War.

No 3217 was built at Swindon works to Lot No 315 which covered 20 locomotives, Nos 3200 to 3219. Completed in March 1938 at a cost of £2398 for the engine and £1016 for the tender, the new machine was officially regarded as a rebuild of 3300 class No 3425.

No 3217 was recorded in Swindon Works B shop on 20th February 1938 as having the frames of No 3425, the boiler (No 3277) and cab of 3252 class No 3282; the remaining parts were from 3252 class No 3258. The tender (No 2032) came from 43xx 2-6-0 No 4334, which was withdrawn in October 1936.

The only Great Western locomotive on the Bluebell Railway, it is one of only two GWR 4-4-0s to be preserved, the other being the record-breaking *City of Truro*, which is part of the National collection.

Briefly, the history of the donor locomotives, something of whose spirit lives on in No 3217, is as follows: No 3258 was built at Swindon (Lot No 101, works No 1498) in September 1895. As built it carried the number 3259 and the name *Lizard*, although this was changed to *The Lizard* in January 1904. It was renumbered 3258 in 1912 and was withdrawn from service in February 1938.

In pristine condition, No 3217 not long after it was built, carried the GWR 'shirt button' monogram on its tender, when it was recorded at Aberystwyth on 8th April 1939.
Steamchest collection

No 3282 was completed at Swindon in March 1899 (Lot No 113, works No 1684). It was originally numbered 3314 and carried the name *Chepstow Castle*. Renumbered again, to 3282 in 1912, in 1923 lost its name to one of the first batch of Collett's 'Castle' class 4-6-0s, No 4077. No 3282 was withdrawn in October 1937.

The final donor of parts to No 3217 was No 3425 built in 1906 (Lot No 162, works No 2138) as No 3715. Renumbered No 3425 in 1912, this locomotive was never given a name and was withdrawn in February 1938.

The new 4-4-0s were known, for obvious reasons, as the 'Dukedogs'. Allocated new to Aberystwyth shed, No 3217 spent its life working on the former Cambrian lines in Wales. It was renumbered 9017 on 29th August 1946.

Its last heavy general overhaul in BR service was at Stafford Road Works, Wolverhampton. It entered the works on 24th August 1955, returning to traffic on 7th October 1955, during which time it was fitted with boiler No 3205, which it retained through into preservation.

No 9017 was withdrawn from service by British Railways on 25th October 1960 having completed a mileage of 422,597. With sister locomotive No 9014, withdrawn on the same day, they were the last of the class to survive, and, apart from 'City' class 4-4-0 No 3717 (3440) *City of Truro,* already in preservation, were the last outside framed locomotives in service in Europe.

The name *Earl of Berkeley* carried in preservation was allotted to No 3217, but was never

carried during its service on the GWR or BR. The story has often been told that certain members of the aristocracy objected to their titles being borne by such ancient looking machines as the 'Dukedog' class. Whether this is true or not the name *Earl of Berkeley* was certainly carried by 'Castle' class 5060.

After withdrawal, No 9017 was stored at Oswestry Works following its sale for the sum of £1,549 to Mr T R Gomm of Birmingham. The purchase price included the two nameplates 'Earl of Berkeley'. When No 5060 was withdrawn in April 1963, its nameplates were placed on No 3217, as had been the original intention.

No 9017 was despatched under its own steam to Old Oak Common shed, London, on the 14th of February 1962, and delivered to the

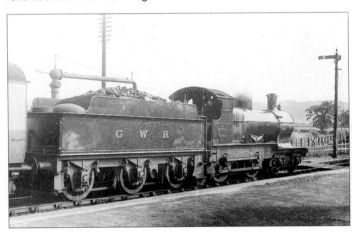

Above: **Though it was not officially renumbered until 29th August 1946, No 9017 carried her new identity as early as the 17th August. It is seen here at Moat Lane Junction on 24th August 1948, working the 7.40 am service from Aberystwyth.** H C Casserley

Above right: **A very clean No 9017 rests between duties at Machynlleth shed.** Jim Peden

Right: **In her last years from 1956 to 1960, No 9017 spent most of her time in store. The locomotive was generally only needed from June to September in those years when the Cambrian lines were at their busiest with holiday traffic and special excursions. No 9017 rests in the excursion platform at Barmouth in August 1957.**
N C Simmons courtesy Hugh Davies

Bluebell Railway on the following day. In preservation, tender No 1805 was replaced with one numbered 1840, built December 1911, and which had never been attached to a 'Dukedog' during its lifetime.

Right: No 9017 is seen double-heading 43xx 2-6-0 No 7330, the latter in unlined green livery, on an excursion out of Shrewsbury in 1960. M Mensing

Below: This pleasing study of No 9017 is believed to have been taken at Pwllheli shed in the late 1950s. R L Inns collection

No 30064

The story of 'USA' 0-6-0 tank No 30064 is a continuation of the history of the steam dock tank in Southampton Docks and follows that of the Bluebell's B4 class 0-4-0T (see pages 11 to 13).

Shunting activities at the busy docks in Southampton were steam dominated by two types of steam locomotives from the 1890s onwards. By a quirk of BRs numbering system we will deal with the later type first. Before tracing No 30064's career it is worth noting that from 1893 to 1977 a constant total of 14 engines were required to work the dock lines there. From 1893 to 1947 the B4 0-4-0 tanks were used and from

1947 to 1962 USA 0-6-0 tanks Nos 61 to 74 were in use. These were replaced by 14 275 hp 0-6-0 diesel shunters, Nos D2985 to D2998, which were employed from 1962 to 1977.

Between 1942 and 1944 large numbers of 0-6-0 tank locomotives were built in the USA for the Ministry of Supply. At least 438 were constructed by three contractors. Many of these were delivered to the UK, the Continent and the Middle East. By 1945 many of the B4 class 0-4-0Ts were in need of new boilers. Both on grounds of cost and because post-war shortages of materials would have led to lengthy delays in the refurbishment of the B4s, O V S Bulleid, Chief Mechanical Engineer of the SR, decided to replace them. At that time quantities

of both British and American War Department locomotives were stored in dumps at Longmoor and Newbury Racecourse, respectively. These were considered as a source of replacements for the B4s, preference being given to the American locomotives.

The future BR No 30064 was built by the Vulcan Iron works, Wilkes-Barre, Philadelphia, USA, (works No 4432) in February 1943. It was given the WD Transportation Corps number 1959. Brought to England, it was initially sent to the Melbourne branch in Leicestershire. From the latter part of 1945 until well into 1947 it was one of 46 in store at Newbury Racecourse.

The Southern Railway took fifteen of the American 0-6-0Ts into stock in May 1946.

As SR No 64, our locomotive entered service in the week ending 22nd June 1947. Seen at Southampton Docks on 21st September 1947, just visible behind the front of the engine is one of the B4 0-4-0Ts it was to replace, No 95 *Honfleur*.
H C Casserley

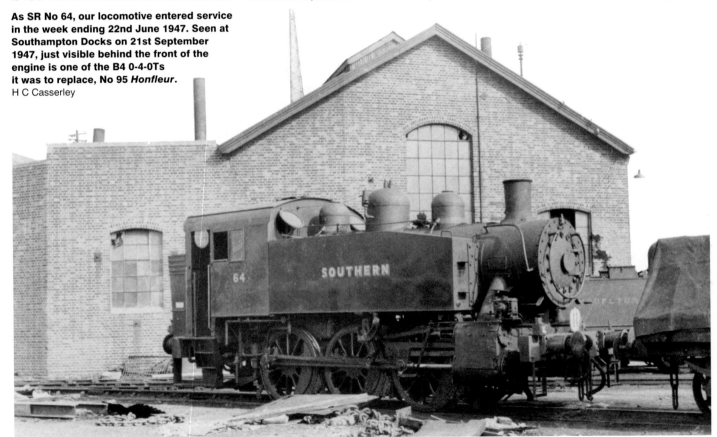

Approval for their purchase, at a cost of £2,500 each, was given on 18th December 1946. Fourteen locomotives were operating in Southampton Docks by the end of November 1947. The fifteenth locomotive was used as a source of spare parts for the others.

Upon Nationalisation the legend 'British Railways' was applied to the tank sides and its number was prefixed with the letter 's', becoming No s64 in February 1948. The locomotive emerged from Eastleigh works in the week ending 15th March 1952, having been fitted with new British-designed boiler mountings, the first variety of BR totem and her new number, 30064.

In May 1955 No 30064 was fitted with a radio telephone to allow more efficient use of the engine in the Docks complex. The locomotive continued to work at Southampton Docks until 1962, when the dock work was taken over by BR class 07 Ruston & Hornsby 275 hp 0-6-0 diesel shunters.

No 30064 was transferred to Eastleigh shed in June 1963. All of the locomotive's repairs had been carried out at Eastleigh Works from the time of its acquisition by the SR. Its last general repair was undertaken between 30th December 1963 and 8th February 1964, when it emerged repainted in lined malachite green livery. No 30064 was in regular use as a pilot at Eastleigh Locomotive and Carriage works and at the shed and also saw service at Guildford, until it was transferred for use at Meldon Quarry,

near Okehampton, in August 1966. The quarry had passed from Southern to Western Region control at the end of 1965. No 30064 had the unlikely distinction of becoming the Western Region's last active steam locomotive from August to October 1966, when a diesel shunter took over at the quarry. Reallocated back to Eastleigh shed in October 1966, the locomotive remained in service until the cessation of steam operations on the Southern Region in July 1967. Her mileage on withdrawal was 301,093.

No 30064 was sold in December 1967. It was moved to Droxford and then to Liss, whilst owned by the Southern Preservation Company Limited and arrived on the Bluebell Railway on 24th October 1971.

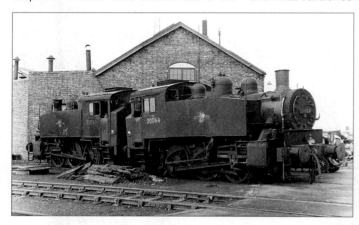

Above left: **In this photograph No 30064 is seen in company with sister locomotive No 30067 parked at the Docks shed. Both now carry the second variety of BR totem. The date is about 1958.** W A C Smith

Above right: **Immaculate in the lined malachite green livery applied at her last overhaul in 1964, No 30064 is seen here at Eastleigh shed having just emerged from the works.** R L Inns collection

Left: **No 30064 was photographed in May 1967, again at Eastleigh, only two months before the cessation of steam operations on the Southern Region.** J G Dewing

No 30096

In the 19th century the quays and sidings at Southampton Docks were worked by horses for a number of years before steam locomotives were regularly used from 1878 onwards. When ownership of the docks passed to the L&SWR in December 1891 it also inherited a fleet of seven tank engines.

As a result of the increasing traffic being generated as the port expanded, four Adams B4 class 0-4-0 tank engines were transferred there in December 1893.

The first order of B4 tanks, dated 6th August 1890, described this class as 'Small Tram Engines'. They were built as specialist shunting tanks and were associated with Southampton Docks as the standard shunting tank from 1893 to 1947, working primarily in the Old Docks. Twenty-five of the class were built, in three batches between October 1891 and June 1908.

Normandy was built at the L&SWR's Nine Elms works in London, to Order No D6. It had the Nine Elms works number 396. It was completed in November 1893, being named and fitted with a cutaway backplate to its cab to improve the crew's visibility when running in reverse, from new. It was painted in L&SWR lined green livery. The number 96 was applied in

December 1893, the month it arrived at Southampton. Fourteen of the B4 tanks were eventually sent to work there.

Normandy was named in accordance with an old tradition of the Southampton Dock Company, the names of whose engines were of continental origin. In the 1920s the locomotive's

Our earliest view of *Normandy* is at the shed in Southampton Docks. Taken by H C Casserley on 12th August 1928 it shows the cutaway cab backplate to good effort. The footplate of a B4 must have been a cold place to do a day's work when the wind was gusting in from the Solent.

livery was unlined dark green. From late 1935 this was changed to unlined black. Modifications over the years included the extension to the rear of its original cutaway cab, provided to comply with wartime blackout conditions and a stovepipe chimney carried in the 1940s.

After the war 'USA' tanks were drafted into Southampton Docks to take over from the B4s which were transferred to other locations. No 96 went first to Eastleigh shed in 1948. In August 1949 it was transferred to Ashford shed. Whilst there it was used for shunting duties at Chislet Colliery in the Kent coalfield. It returned to Eastleigh in March 1950 where it remained until its withdrawal. Under BR it was renumbered 30096 and lost its name in December 1950.

By 1960 No 30096 could be seen occasionally at work in its old haunts at Southampton Docks. In September of that year it was sharing shunting duties at Winchester with sister locomotive No 30102 (now the only other member of this class preserved). No 30096 was the last B4 to be overhauled by BR, at Eastleigh Works, the work being completed in March 1961. At that time it had the second variety of BR totem applied, the only member of the class to carry this. It was displayed at Eastleigh Works Open Day on 1st August 1962 along with T9 4-4-0 No 120 'Merchant Navy' class 4-6-2 No 35022, both of which were subsequently preserved, and an example of the latest variety of Southampton Docks shunter, diesel 0-6-0 No D2990, built only the previous month.

No 30096 was withdrawn from service in the week ending 6th October 1963, with a total mileage of 483,917. A Drewry diesel shunter arrived to replace the B4 on its duties at Winchester goods yard. The locomotive was sold in December 1963 to Corralls Limited, fuel merchants, to replace their Peckett 0-4-0ST *Bristol*. It was named *Corrall Queen* and worked at Dibles Wharf in Southampton. From 1964 to 1969 it was employed shunting wagons at the wharf and conveying wagons twice a day to the BR exchange sidings at Northam.

It was purchased for preservation at a cost of £1,000 by the Bulleid Society and delivered to the Bluebell Railway during the afternoon of Tuesday 19th December 1972.

Top: **Upon the arrival of their successors, the USA tanks, the B4 tanks were transferred away, No 96 going to Easteigh shed where it was photographed on 2nd October 1948. The stovepipe chimney seen on the previous page had been replaced by the more elegant Drummond type in March 1948.** S C Nash

Above: **Her BR numberplate, Easteigh shed plate and her new *Corrall Queen* name plates adorn the loco at Dibles Wharf in Southampton on 2nd January 1971.** Steamchest collection

Opposite page, top: ***Normandy* is shunting banana vans in this scene in the Docks taken around 1930.** R C Stumpf collection

Opposite page, bottom: **In this picture, probably taken in the late 1940s, No 96 *Normandy* sports her stovepipe chimney. The World War II modifications to her cab can also be seen.** R C Stumpf collection

Above: **No 96 *Normandy* is shunting at Southampton Docks on 13th September 1936.** H F Wheeler collection, courtesy R S Carpenter

Below: **No 30096 was recorded shunting the goods yard on 24th June 1961.** J C Haydon

No 30541

The Q class 0-6-0 was the last of Richard Maunsell's designs for the Southern Railway. It was intended as a replacement for the ageing Western Section 'Jubilee' class 0-4-2 locomotives, then still in use on middle-distance traffic.

An order for 20 locomotives, Nos 530 to 549, was placed in March 1936. They were constructed at Eastleigh works at a cost of £7,200 each. The cost included 20 new boilers at £1,525 each, and twenty 4,000 gallon tenders intended for use with N and U class locomotives. The new Q would then receive second-hand 3,500 gallon tenders from the Moguls. By the time the class entered service O V S Bulleid had taken over from Maunsell as Chief Mechanical Engineer on the SR.

No 541 was completed in January 1939 and allocated to Guildford shed. It was painted in black livery, which it retained during its entire working life, and was equipped with 3,500 gallon tender No 1909, previously attached to U class 2-6-0 No 1619. No 541 is still paired with this tender today. At Guildford it worked goods trains much of the time over the Redhill to Guildford line.

In 1942 it was derailed near Betchworth as a result of an enemy bomb exploding near the line, seriously damaging its boiler and firebox. Later that year as a result of the arrival of new class Q1 0-6-0s at Guildford shed, Q class Nos 541 to 544 were transferred to Horsham, and were the first of the class to be allocated to a shed off the Western Section. On the Central Section they were employed on a variety of services, including passenger trains.

Repairs to the class were normally carried out at Eastleigh Works between 1942 and 1945, but in 1942 to 1945 No 541 was dealt with at Ashford. At the end of 1946 No 541 became the seventh member of the class to have its distinctive Maunsell chimney replaced by one of large diameter, and the locomotive was equipped with a Lemâitre multiple jet blastpipe. All 20 of the class were so treated as part of Bulleid's attempt to remedy a draughting problem that had hampered their performance.

In December 1947 No 541 was transferred to Three Bridges shed, and was regularly used on services into London Bridge. In September 1948 it was renumbered 30541 by British Railways. It moved shed twice in 1953, first in June to Stewarts Lane and then in September to Bournemouth Central where it remained for nine years and was a regular sight along many South Coast routes.

Two months after the end of hostilities in Europe, No 541 stands outside the shed at Norwood Junction on 28th July 1945.
H C Casserley

In January 1963, No 30541 was transferred to Basingstoke, and in March to Guildford. At this time it was relegated to local goods duties and engineering trains. At Eastleigh Works in March 1963 it was fitted with brackets for attaching snowploughs.

No 30541 was the 14th member of the class to be withdrawn from service, in the week ending 29th November 1964. Sold to Woodham Brothers, for scrapping, it was towed by No 34051 from Eastleigh via Westbury to Barry on 23rd February 1965, in the company of Nos 34045 and 34105.

Purchased for preservation on 21st September 1973 for £3,250, it was the 54th locomotive to leave the Barry scrapyard, being moved by road in May 1974 to a temporary home at the Dowty Railway Preservation Society headquarters at Ashchurch in Gloucestershire. It left Ashchurch by road on 5th October 1978, had an overnight sojourn at Caterham, and was delivered the following day to the Bluebell Railway.

No 541 at Bournemouth shed in the Autumn of 1963, having just worked a service from Brockenhurst via Wimborne. Bournemouth Central station is visible in the background. R Blencowe collection

At Chatham station on 26th July 1953. No 30541, carrying a Stewarts Lane shedplate, is hauling nine-coach 'birdcage' set No 900 forming the 10.50 am excursion from Victoria to Sheerness-on-Sea. On the right of the picture is a 1939 built 2-HAL electric multiple unit, No 2625. N W Spinks

No 30583

The '415' class was designed by William Adams, who was appointed Chief Mechanical Engineer of the London & South Western Railway on 17th January 1878.

The design was based to a large extent upon the existing L&SWR '46' class 4-4-0 tanks, known as the 'Ironclads'. The '415' class 4-4-2 tanks were particularly fine-looking engines and possibly among the most handsome of tank engines built in the Victorian era. Seventy-one locomotives of the class were constructed between August 1882 and December 1885 by four outside contractors.

Twelve of the class passed directly from the L&SWR to the Southern Railway at the Grouping in 1923. This is the history of a thirteenth member of the class which the SR only acquired in 1946.

No 488 was built in March 1885 by Neilson & Company in Glasgow, their works No 3209. The cost of building the eleven locomotives of the batch, Nos 479 to 489 inclusive, was £2,580 each. No 488 was the 50th member of the class completed. At first it worked suburban services in the London area to destinations such as Epsom, Leatherhead, Guildford, Hampton Court, Windsor, Reading and Basingstoke.

The transfer of the class to the L&SWR Duplicate List began in 1904; No 488 was so transferred in March 1914 and renumbered 0488. It was laid aside at Eastleigh Works for scrapping. However with the commencement of hostilities in the First World War it was reprieved and reinstated in traffic.

In September 1917 it was withdrawn from service, the second member of the class to go, the first being No 424 in June 1916. The locomotive was sold to the Government for £2,104. Overhauled at Eastleigh Works during October, it was painted dark green and numbered 27. It then saw service with the Ministry of Munitions at the General Salvage Depot, Ridham Dock, near Sittingbourne in Kent. It was sold again for £900 in April 1919 to the East Kent Light Railway, who numbered it 5. On the East Kent Light Railway, No 5 was last repaired in 1937. From March 1939 it lay derelict at Shepherdswell.

The Lyme Regis branch in Dorset, which was opened on Monday 24th August 1903, became synonymous with the Adams '415' class 4-4-2 tanks. The severe curvature of the branch made the short wheel base Adams 4-4-2Ts ideal engines to work it. Three of the class were introduced there in 1914. In October 1928 the two remaining on the line were out of service needing heavy repairs. By this time their sisters on the SR had been withdrawn. Trials with other classes proved unsuccessful so in the summer of 1930 the two laid aside were reprieved and overhauled.

By 1946 the two Lyme Regis branch engines, Nos 3125 and 3520, required heavy overhauls.

Opposite page top: **As EKR No 5, at Shepherdswell shed in 1927, the locomotive still retains L&SWR style livery. Behind is EKR No 1, an ex-GWR saddle tank.** H C Casserley collection

Opposite page bottom: **No 5, newly overhauled and painted, with No 4, a Kerr Stuart 'Victory' class 0-6-0T, at Shepherdswell on 18th July 1936.** H C Casserley

This page right: **SR No 3488 hauling a rake of three ex-L&SWR bogie carriages, forming the down 1.45 pm train to Lyme Regis, is seen leaving Axminster on 25th June 1949. The concrete spikes to the left of the track are anti-tank devices dating from 1940.** The Lyon collection

Below: **As SR No 3488 in Eastleigh Works yard on 14th August 1949 awaiting overhaul and renumbering The engine is parked between a B4 class 0-4-0T and the Drummond tender of a 4-4-0.** W Gilburt, courtesy Steamchest collection

No 3488 at its home shed, Exmouth Junction, probably during 1949.
R C Stumpf collection

Below: **No 30583 arrives at Lyme Regis with a train from Axminster on 11th June 1960. The stock is formed of a Maunsell brake/third and an open third. Note the small sub-shed for the branch engines on the right.** L G Marshall

Following overhaul in late August and September 1949 at Eastleigh works, it returned to traffic as BR No 30583. The locomotive is the centre of attention at Tipton St Johns on 12th April 1953, when hauling a railtour from Exeter Central to Exmouth, which returned to Exeter via Sidmouth Junction. N W Spinks

Whilst the two engines could continue to handle the traffic, the SR considered that a third engine was needed so it was decided to purchase EKR No 5. The price was £800, though some sources say the 4-4-2T cost as little as £120.

EKR No 5 was hauled by SR class N 2-6-0 No 1811 from Ashford to Eastleigh on 15th March 1946. At Eastleigh Works it was overhauled and fitted with the spare Drummond boiler, No 916, which itself dated back to 1907. It was taken into SR stock as No 3488 on 13th August 1946 and arrived in the West Country in December 1946. The three locomotives then worked a week at a time on the branch, the changeover taking place on Saturdays. The roster actually allowed for a second engine to provide assistance on summer Saturdays to pilot trains containing through coaches off the Waterloo expresses. The third member of the trio was then either spare or, if necessary, away at Eastleigh Works for repairs.

All three class '415' engines passed into BR ownership. No 3488 was overhauled at Eastleigh Works, leaving in September 1949 painted in lined black livery and bearing its new number, 30582. On 26th February 1954 it visited Newton Abbot Works for weighing purposes, the first recorded visit of the type there.

Two Drummond boilers, Nos 916 and 921, with safety valves mounted on their domes, constructed in 1907, had been carried alternately on the locomotive between August 1946 and March 1959. During its last major overhaul by British Railways in March 1959, it was fitted with an Adams pattern boiler.

Withdrawal of all three of the class came in 1961. No 30583 was the penultimate of the trio to be withdrawn from service in the week ending 22nd July 1961, No 30582 surviving it by a week. When No 30583 was withdrawn it must have had one of the highest ever mileages recorded for a British steam locomotive. The total of 1,604,703 was broken down as follows; 1,230,696 on the L&SWR, 72,165 on the EKLR, and 301,842 for the SR/BR.

One of the Adams tanks was an eminently suitable candidate for preservation. No 30583 was chosen because it carried the Adams pattern boiler. It left the Lyme Regis branch on 8th July 1961 for Brighton, and was delivered to Sheffield Park on the Bluebell Railway on the 12th of that month. Its purchase price was £850 – just a little bit more than the SR had first paid the East Kent in 1946.

No 30583 double-heads sister locomotive No 30584 near Combpyne with through coaches from Waterloo bound for Lyme Regis on 8th August 1959. J G Dewing

No 30830

The S15 class 4-6-0 was introduced in 1920, designed by R W Urie of the London & South Western Railway. Intended mainly for long-distance freight duties, a further series of these locomotives was built under the direction of Richard Maunsell of the Southern Railway. His engines incorporated modifications to the original Urie design, having straight running plates, outside steampipes and Maunsell cabs and chimneys.

No 830 was built at Eastleigh Works to Order No E90, authorised on 1st May 1925. This was for ten locomotives, Nos 823 to 832, which were delivered between March 1927 and January 1928. Our locomotive was completed in August 1927 at a cost of £10,415 and was allocated to Salisbury shed. Its livery from new until July 1939 was standard Maunsell green, with black and white lining. Initially numbered E830, the 'E' prefix was discontinued after 1931. Smoke deflectors were fitted in the first half of 1937. After August 1939 it was painted in dark green, with black and yellow lining. This new style incorporated the number on the cabside and the word 'Southern' on the tender.

In March 1950 it was renumbered 30830 by BR from which time its livery was always goods black. On 3rd December 1955 it worked tender-first hauling the Exmouth branch goods. During a non-classified repair at Eastleigh Works from 20th to 28th May 1960, Automatic Warning System equipment was fitted. In January 1963 the Salisbury to Exeter line became part of the Western Region, which regarded it as a secondary route. Following the takeover and after spending all of its life shedded at Salisbury, No 30830 was reallocated to Feltham shed in the January of 1964,

Withdrawn from service on 26th July 1964, the locomotive had run up a creditable mileage of 1,259,236. In mid September 1964 it was in store with 29 other steam locomotives at Eastleigh shed, and by the beginning of December 1964 it had been moved to Salisbury.

No 830 with a train of ex-L&SWR non-corridor bogie stock forming a Waterloo to Salisbury service enters Clapham Junction on 21st July 1937.
J P Wilson courtesy The Lyon collection

Pacifics Nos 34027 and 35018 were towed by No 34064 through Basingstoke to Salisbury on 7th December 1964. Later that day, Nos 30830 and 35006 were collected there and all were then removed to Woodham Brothers' scrapyard at Barry, in South Wales.

In March 1929 its original 5,000 gallon tender was transferred to 'Lord Nelson' class 4-6-0 No E860. To replace it, No E830 received another 5,000 gallon tender previously fitted to N15 class 'King Arthur' 4-6-0 No E765. This replacement tender, originally numbered 882 subsequently renumbered 3227, was retained from then until the locomotive was sent to the scrapyard, where it was detached and sold for use with sister engine No 30828 when that machine was preserved.

No 30830 was purchased for preservation by the Maunsell Locomotive Society in the summer of 1987 without a tender. Delivered to the Bluebell Railway on 23rd September 1987, it became the 192nd locomotive to leave the Barry scrapyard, having spent 22 years and 9 months there.

Above right: **No 30830, in passenger service on a Salisbury to Exeter stopping train, is seen near Templecombe on 6th September 1963.** D M C Hepburne-Smith

Below: **No 30830, on the sort of duty for which it was built, powers a freight along the Southern Region's West of England main line in the early 1950s.** Pursey Short, courtesy Mike Esau

No 30847

A second member of the useful S15 class 4-6-0s No 847, has found sanctuary on the Bluebell Railway. No 847 was the last of ten S15s, Nos 838 to 847, built at Eastleigh Works to Order No E630 between May and December 1936. Completed in December 1936, it entered service on the 30th of that month, and was the last 4-6-0 constructed for the Southern Railway. Built

at a cost of £14,145, it was allocated new to Exmouth Junction shed.

Bulleid's livery changes did not greatly affect the Urie and Maunsell S15s. Turned out in 1936 in green livery with black and white lining; following its first general overhaul in July 1939, by which time it had covered a total of 107,139 miles, No 847 returned to traffic in green, lined out in black and yellow. In June 1942 it was repainted in austere wartime unlined black.

Following Nationalisation in August 1948, it was renumbered 30847 and painted goods black. During its allocation to Exmouth Junction it was mostly used on long-distance freights and secondary passenger trains. In June 1951 it was

Left: **No 847 in later Southern Railway livery, with the number on the cabsides was at Chard Junction in August 1947. It is working a stopping service to Exeter. The tender is the 8-wheel flat-sided 5,000 gallon type, which was fitted from new.** Roger Venning, courtesy Mike Esau

transferred to Salisbury shed, where it continued to be used on main-line goods, but also stopping passenger trains to Waterloo, and between Salisbury, Templecombe, Axminster and Exeter Central.

In June 1959 No 847 was moved from Salisbury to Redhill shed. The locomotive had been fitted from new with an 8-wheel flat-sided 5,000 gallon tender. In April 1960, because the Central Section's turntables were slightly smaller, its tender was exchanged for a 3,500 six-wheel tender No 914, from N15 class 4-6-0 No 30797 *Sir Blamor de Ganis*. Tender No 914 eventually accompanied No 30847 to Woodham's scrapyard. From there it was sold to the Mid-Hants Railway, to work with their U class Mogul, No 31806. Also in June 1960 No 30847 was fitted with boiler No 456, which was constructed in April 1925 for 'King Arthur' class 4-6-0 No 456. Prior to fitting to No 30847 it was, from October 1955, on the now preserved 'King Arthur' class 4-6-0 No 30777 *Sir Lamiel*.

Withdrawn from service on 5th January 1964, the same date as the H class 0-4-4T No 31263, also preserved on the Bluebell Railway, No 30847's final mileage was 931,829. It was sold to Woodham Bros at Barry, leaving Feltham shed on 18th June 1964 for the last time. S15 class 4-6-0 No 30506 towed sister engines Nos 30499, 30841 and 30847 (all four of which were subsequently preserved) from Feltham, but unfortunately No 30506 failed at Staines and had to return light engine to Feltham. Another S15, No 30824, then towed No 30506, picking up the other three at Staines and brought all four via Eastleigh to Newport, en route to Barry.

No 30847 was purchased for preservation at a cost of £9,000 plus VAT on 12th September 1978. It was the 94th locomotive to leave the Barry scrapyard. No 30847 together with tender No 3225 from S15 No 30828, and Standard class 4 2-6-4T No 80100, all left Barry in October 1978 for a new phase in their careers on the Bluebell Railway.

Left: **Near Templecombe, No 847 is hauling a train of ex-L&SWR corridor bogie stock and a PMV van in 1947.** R L Inns collection

No 30847, hauls an up Salisbury to Waterloo stopping train, formed of Maunsell Restriction 1 stock, near Winchfield on 16th May 1953. K W Wightman, courtesy The Lyon collection

No 30847, now with six-wheel tender No 914 in tow, hauls a fitted freight near Basingstoke about 1962. Steamchest collection

Below: **Stored at Feltham after withdrawal, No 30847 is buffered up to one of Bulleid's Q1 class 0-6-0s. In the background are H16 class 4-6-2T No 30518, built in 1921 and withdrawn in November 1962, and a W class 2-6-4T. Whilst several S15s have been preserved, no example of either of these SR tank engine classes cheated the scrapman.** Lens of Sutton

No 30928 *Stowe*

Designed by R E L Maunsell, the 'Schools' class 4-4-0 was a cut-down version of the 'Lord Nelson' class, having one pair of driving wheels less and only three cylinders. They were built to handle intermediate express duties for which, up to 1927, no modern class existed. Maunsell had envisaged large-wheeled 2-6-4 tanks fulfilling this role, but the derailment of class K 2-6-4T A800 *River Cray* at Sevenoaks on 24th August 1927 forced him to consider other alternatives. His solution to the problem was to produce a large and powerful 4-4-0 capable of hauling all but the heaviest expresses. The Southern Railway's dynamic publicity department proclaimed the type, at the time of their introduction, as the most powerful 4-4-0 in Europe. Much interest was aroused by the revival of the 4-coupled type for mainline work, in view of the general preference for 6-coupled types at the time. All 40 of the class were constructed at Eastleigh Works.

No 928 was built to Order No E403 of March 1931 which covered the 20 locomotives, Nos 910 to 929. The average cost of building this order was £5,374. It entered traffic in June 1934 allocated to Fratton shed and was used on Waterloo to Portsmouth services. It was fitted with smoke-deflectors from new, and carried a single blastpipe throughout its entire working life.

The Southern Railway had a policy of naming its express locomotives in order to gain publicity and it was decided to name these engines after well known public schools. No 928 was named *Stowe* after the school situated in Buckinghamshire.

All the locomotive's repairs and maintenance were carried out at Eastleigh up to the end of 1956, with the exception of a visit to Brighton Works in April 1947. Its last three repairs were undertaken at Ashford.

In July 1937 it was transferred to Bournemouth shed, where it remained until November 1946. From that time it was at Brighton. In September 1947 No 928 went to Bricklayers Arms in London and in September 1948 it was transferred the short distance to Stewarts Lane. In May 1949 it returned to Bricklayers Arms, remaining there until transferred to its final shed, Brighton, in October 1961.

Renumbered 30928 by British Railways in June 1948, in May 1949 it was rostered by Newhaven Depot to work the 8.18 am Uckfield to Victoria in place of a failed Brighton Atlantic. Official sanction for the 'Schools' class to use this route was not given until 1958!

In May 1961 Nos 30928 and 30934/5/6 appeared at Tonbridge to work the Uckfield line services to Brighton, and they proved very popular with the crews on heavily loaded trains.

Withdrawn from service on 17th November 1962, No 30928 was repainted in Maunsell green livery and displayed, with three Pullman coaches, at the Montagu (now National) Motor Museum, at Beaulieu, in Hampshire.

David Shepherd bought a half-share in the locomotive in Autumn 1972 and it was moved to the East Somerset Railway at Cranmore, Somerset, in November 1973.

One of three members of the class which have been preserved, No 30928 was moved to the Bluebell Railway on 10th July 1980.

No 928, in sage green livery, on a semi-fast Waterloo to Portsmouth train in 1935. The train is formed of ex-L&SWR bogie non-corridor stock. R F Stephens collection

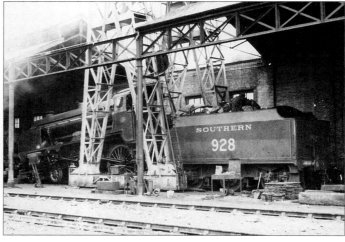

Following transfer to Bournemouth shed in July 1937, the locomotive was soon under repair there on 19th July of that year. The locomotive number is painted on the rear of the tender. H C Casserley

Right: **No 928 is seen in wartime black livery at Eastleigh Works around 1946. Behind is an E1R class 0-6-2T.** Lens of Sutton

Below: **No 30928 hauling a rake of ex-SE&CR bogie birdcage stock, forming a Hastings to Tonbridge stopping train, is seen between West St Leonards and Crowhurst in the summer of 1956.** N W Spinks

Left: **In July 1959 No 30928 was repainted in BR lined green livery with the later variety of BR totem. The locomotive was photographed passing through Paddock Wood on 29th August 1959, hauling the 10.00 am Deal to Charing Cross service, formed of BR Mk.1 stock.** D W Winkworth

Below: **At Stewarts Lane shed on 7th April 1956, No 30928 in lined black livery, carries a 73B Bricklayers Arms shedplate and sports a small version of the early BR 'cycling lion' totem on its tender.** L G Marshall

No 31027

In 1905 and 1906 eight steam railmotors were delivered to the South Eastern & Chatham Railway by Kitsons for use on lightly trafficked branch lines. They were not very successful and were soon replaced by auto-trains worked by a new design of small 0-6-0 tank.

H S Wainwright's P class locomotives were apparently inspired by Stroudley's class A 'Terrier' tanks of the LB&SCR. Wainwright scaled down the dimensions of these locomotives in a desire for economy, to such an extent that they were not powerful enough to perform the work required of them. They did not therefore achieve the same reputation as the 'Terriers'.

Our loco as Southern Railway A27 at Dover Docks, probably in 1928.
P E Simpson, courtesy D Sprange collection

All eight members of the class were built at Ashford Works. The first two, Nos 753 and 754, ordered on 23rd January 1908, entered traffic on 18th and 23rd February 1909, respectively. Nos 27, 178, 323, 325, 555 and 558 were ordered in February 1908, built at an estimated cost of £1,835 each, and entered traffic between February and July 1910.

No 27, the first of the second batch, entered traffic on 19th February 1910. It was allocated new to Sheerness shed and worked on the Isle of Sheppey Light Railway. All of the class were turned out in lined passenger green livery, with polished brasswork, copper-capped chimneys, and Wainwright 'Pagoda' pattern cabs. During the course of No 27's first overhaul at Ashford Works in August and September 1912, the equipment required to work auto-trains was

removed, an early reflection that the class had not been successful on the duties for which it had been intended. In July 1914 it was reallocated to Reading shed.

Two members of the P class, Nos 27 and 753, were shipped to Boulogne on 24th April 1915 on loan to the Railway Operating Division, for local shunting duties. Before departure they were repainted in unvarnished olive green with large yellow numerals on the tank sides beneath the letters ROD. After arrival at Boulogne they were renumbered 5027 and 5753. No 5027 was put to work on the quays and supply depots at Calais. Both were repatriated via the Richborough train ferry on 30th October 1916.

One source states that No 27, on arrival back from France, was repainted in SE&CR grey livery at Dover shed. However the engine history

Above: **In April 1936 the loco was at Ashford Works following a general overhaul. Now numbered 1027, the number was applied to the back of the coal bunker as well as to the tanks.** R L Inns collection

Below: **At Eastleigh on 30th August 1952. The 'shaded' lettering and numerals of the 1948 BR repaint are only just visible, as are the numerals 027 of the 1936 SR repaint.**
R L Inns collection

record card indicates that it underwent a general overhaul at Ashford Works from 31st October to 1st December 1916, which was probably when it received the grey livery.

In January 1917 No 27 was transferred to Folkestone shed, where it remained until June 1945, with the exception of two spells at Dover from late 1927 to July 1928, and in 1937. It received another general overhaul at Ashford Works early in 1919 during which its working pressure was reduced from 180 to 160 psi.

Following the Grouping in 1923, in the course of another general overhaul at Ashford Works in 1926, it was renumbered A27, received attention to its tanks and was repainted lined passenger green.

It received another General overhaul at Ashford works from February to April 1936 during which time new cylinders were fitted, it was painted in unlined green and numbered 1027.

From June 1945 it was reallocated to Dover shed. It became a firm favourite with the locomen there, where it was to spend most of the rest of its career until withdrawal.

During an overhaul at Ashford Works in 1948 it was renumbered as British Railways 31027. In 1951 it was loaned to Betteshanger Colliery. During 1952 it had two periods of storage, in January at Dover and in July at Fratton; before being reallocated to Eastleigh from February to October 1952. It returned to Dover in October 1952. In July 1953 it was again in store at Dover. In 1955 it was allocated to St Leonards shed to act as a standby engine for the Tenterden goods workings on the former K&ESR. In June 1958 it was loaned to the Chislet Colliery.

No 31027's last repair in British Railways ownership was a non-classified one including a boiler washout, at Ashford Works from 21st February to 10th March 1961.

Shortly after leaving the works, No 31027, which had been purchased by the Bluebell Railway, the second member of its class to final sanctuary there, arrived on the line, on 18th March 1961. This was before it was officially withdrawn, at the end of the week ending 25th March, by the other BR. The locomotives' final recorded mileage in her railway service up to withdrawal, was a creditable 523,282 miles.

No 31178

The first three engines of the second batch of the SE&CR P class 0-6-0 tanks to be built have all been preserved on the Bluebell Railway.

No 178 entered traffic on 25th February 1910, painted in lined passenger green livery in common with the rest of the class. Allocated new to Reading shed from 1st March 1910, it assisted sister engine No 754 in working the Reading to Ash and Ash to Aldershot services.

In the period between December 1912 and July 1913 it had its auto-train gear modified at Ashford Works in order to operate with the recently converted motor coach sets Nos 266 to 270, 273 and 274. From 1913 to early 1916, it is believed that it was painted unlined green with large unshaded yellow numerals. In August and September 1913 No 178 was recorded working the Beckenham Junction to Norwood Junction service. It was allocated, with sister locomotives Nos 555 and 558, to Longhedge shed in July 1914 to work the Greenwich Park branch from both Nunhead and Victoria, some services to Crystal Palace (High Level) which came off the main line at Nunhead, and the former LC&DR South London line Victoria to St Pauls service. After 28th July 1914 it was observed working local services between Birchington and Ramsgate Sands.

On 1st December 1915 it was transferred, together with a three-coach motor train, to Hastings for service on the Bexhill branch. In early 1916 it was repainted in grey livery with large numerals in zinc white emblazoned on its tank sides. In March 1916 it was reallocated to Redhill shed for carriage pilot duties. No 178's boiler pressure was reduced to 160 psi and a copper firebox was fitted in January 1917. When this work was completed that month, No 178 was transferred to Bricklayers Arms shed where it was used to shunt the siding at the large Royal Flying Corps Aeronautical Stores Depot at Kidbrooke.

By the time it was transferred to Orpington, on 1st February 1919, to work the Otford shuttle service, its livery was olive green with yellow numerals. In 1920 it was recorded at Folkes-

tone, however by January 1923 it had been moved to Tonbridge, and with a three-coach set, was working on the Westerham branch.

Following the Grouping of 1923, its first general overhaul in Southern Railway ownership was at Ashford Works, where the locomotive arrived on 3rd June 1924. During the course of this works visit the locomotive was renumbered A178 and was repainted in SR dark green livery. In July 1928 it was transferred to Folkestone shed, where it remained until June 1945, with the exception of two short periods at Dover. The locomotive was renumbered again, this time to 1178, during an overhaul at Ashford in October and November 1931.

In June 1945 it was reallocated to Brighton. From 21st January 1948 it underwent an intermediate overhaul at Stewarts Lane depot in London, emerging on 6th March 1948 as British Railways s1178. It was transferred in early 1950 to Dover shed and received another general overhaul at Ashford from March to May 1951, in the course of which the loco was given its final BR number, 31178.

Back at Dover in October 1951 trials comparing No 31178 with B4 class 0-4-0T No 30084 were carried out at the Eastern Docks due to increasing loads which were needing to be moved there. During the Summer of 1953 No

31178 was hired to Bowaters' Lloyd Pulp and Paper Mills Limited at Ridham Dock, near Sittingbourne, when their 0-4-0 saddle tank *Jubilee* was under repair. During 1955 No 31178 was loaned to Chislet Colliery. Later in that year it was reallocated to Bricklayers Arms shed in London, for possible use in the Stores siding on the Deptford Wharf branch. When No 31178 failed on 12th March 1956 it was replaced there by 'Terrier' No 32670. By 23rd April 1956 it had been reallocated to Brighton shed and in September 1957 it was transferred to Stewarts Lane, where it remained until withdrawal. The locomotive received its last general overhaul at Ashford between 10th January and 2nd February 1957.

No 31178 was withdrawn from traffic in the week ending 7th June 1958 with a final mileage of 516,165. It was sold to Bowaters at Sittingbourne, to whom it had been hired during 1953. There it was named *Pioneer II*.

It was acquired from Bowaters for use on the Bluebell Railway and delivered to its new home on 14th October 1969.

No 178 in its wartime grey livery which dated from 1916. R C Stumpf collection

Left: **The locomotive is seen in its fourth livery of olive green which it carried from 1919 to June 1924.**
W Beckerlegge, R L Inns collection

Below: **A178 on shed on 30th July 1925. Alongside it is one of the ill-fated K class 2-6-4Ts, A793** *River Ouse*, **constructed in May 1925 and converted to a class U 2-6-0 tender engine in June 1928 following the accident involving sister loco A800** *River Cray* **near Sevenoaks in August 1927.** R F Stephens collection

Right: **Within three weeks of being repainted in Southern Railway livery, A178 is seen on a Sevenoaks (Tubs Hill) to Bat & Ball push-pull train on 9th August 1924.** Keith Ladbury

Below: **No 1178 is seen here at an unidentified location, carrying its second Southern Railway livery and number, which it received in November 1931.** John Scott-Morgan collection

Above: **No 1178's later SR livery, which it carried from October 1943, is illustrated here. The number was moved to the sides of the bunker at this time.** Steamchest collection

Above: **In its final BR livery carried from May 1951, No 31178 is pictured here at Brighton on 2nd September 1956.** L G Marshall

Below: **This view of the locomotive in its first British Railways livery as s1178, with 'shaded' lettering and numbers, was probably taken in mid-1948.** R L Inns collection

No 31263

H S Wainwright was appointed Locomotive and Carriage Superintendent to the South Eastern & Chatham Railway on 27th September 1898. Drawings were prepared during the last quarter of 1903 under the guidance of Robert Surtees, Chief Draughtsman, for the medium-sized 0-4-4 tank locomotive which became known as the H class. Intended for use on the SE&CR's intensive suburban services, a novelty of the design was the shape of the cab roof, often referred to as the 'pagoda', which was intended to stop rain trickling down off its top. A total of 66 members of the class were built, all at Ashford Works, between 1904 and 1915.

No 263 was completed on 5th May 1905 and allocated new to Slades Green shed, where it remained for five years. It was used on North Kent services, also on additional summertime trains to Ramsgate and Dover, via Faversham, at weekends. Its original livery was lined Brunswick green. From the Autumn of 1915 the engine was turned out in unlined green with unshaded yellow numerals on the tank sides.

After Grouping the locomotive was renumbered A263 and was turned out in SR green livery with yellow lining in December 1923 from Ashford Works. Renumbered 1263 by the summer of 1941, the engine was working out of Nine Elms shed on empty coaching stock duties between Waterloo and Clapham Junction carriage sidings. All but two members of the H class passed into BR ownership. As BR No 31263 its

livery was lined black. The engine moved around many sheds in its BR days, including Redhill in 1955, Ashford in 1956, Tonbridge in March 1960, Tunbridge Wells West in September 1962 and Three Bridges in September 1963.

The last three members of the class, Nos 31263, 31518 and 31551, were withdrawn together at Three Bridges on 5th January 1964. The final mileage of No 31263 was 1,641,825.

Purchased by the H Class Trust, No 31263 was first stored at Robertsbridge moving in 1970 to the South Eastern Steam Centre at Ashford. Following the closure of that site the Trust moved the loco to the Bluebell Railway where it arrived on 25th January 1976.

No 1263 is seen at Dover on 25th June 1939 in olive green livery with black and white lining. H C Casserley

Opposite page: **Though No 31263 had been transferred from Ashford to Tonbridge shed in March 1960, the loco was still carrying an Ashford (74A) shedplate when seen leaving Wateringbury whilst working the 3.08pm Maidstone to Tonbridge service on 29th June 1960. The train consists of ex-SE&CR 'birdcage' stock. As can be seen in the photograph on page 33, the engine had a flat sided bunker from new. This was changed in the early BR period, after 1949, to the curved top bunker side plates, seen in these later pictures.** R L Inns collection

Right: **Three months after withdrawal No 31263 is stored out of use at Three Bridges shed on 25th April 1964.** A Linaker, courtesy Mike Esau

Below: **Hauling a Maunsell designed auto-train set, No 31263 pauses at Rowfant whilst working a Three Bridges to East Grinstead service in June 1963.** R L Inns collection

No 31323

No 323 is a sister locomotive of Wainright's P class Nos 27 and 178 (see pages 27 to 32). This was the fifth member of the class, the third locomotive of the second batch to be built. It was delivered and running trials by 26th April 1910. However it was then stored in the Ashford Works paintshop until 16th July 1910 when it was allocated to Orpington shed and used on the Otford to Sevenoaks service. It was observed working the Beckenham Junction to Norwood Junction service in September 1910 and also used on the Gravesend West branch until well into 1916.

No 323 was painted in passenger green livery when new, but in 1916 this was replaced by unlined grey with large numerals in zinc white. The boiler working pressure was reduced to 160 psi at this time.

In January 1917 it was allocated to Margate shed and by Armistice Day in 1918 it was at Tonbridge shed. It worked services between Hastings and Rye from September 1919 until they ceased completely in 1921. By January 1923 it was working the Otford to Sevenoaks service again, which it continued to do until this line was electrified. The locomotive was also often seen on the Westerham branch. Late in 1926 it was on the books of Dover shed.

No 323 received a general (class A) overhaul at Ashford Works from 18th August 1926 until 8th January 1927, during which it was renumbered as Southern Railway A323, and painted in lined green livery.

No 323 is still carrying SE&CR unlined grey livery when photographed three years after Grouping at Sevenoaks (Tubs Hill) station, at the head of a motor-train to Otford on 3rd April 1926. H C Casserley

No 323 at Sevenoaks (Tubs Hill) Station in 1926. D Sprange collection

Below: **No 1323 at Brighton shed on 23rd April 1939. Behind is D1 class 0-4-2T No 2625, originally LB&SCR No 25 *Rotherfield*.** W A Camwell

Repainted in lined SR green livery in January 1927, A323 was seen at Folkestone Junction on 14th May of that year. H C Casserley

From July 1928 A323 was allocated to Folkestone shed.

In the course of another general overhaul at Ashford Works during July and August 1931 the engine received new cylinders and a new identity, No 1323. In July 1933 it was allocated to Dover shed and in early 1938 to Brighton. In September 1943 No 1323 was loaned to Snowdown Colliery, near Canterbury, though by 20th February 1945 it was back at Folkestone shed. Between the end of the Second World War and Nationalisation it had some long periods in storage.

No 1323 entered Ashford Works on 12th January 1949 for a light intermediate overhaul. It emerged from the works bearing its final identity, as British Railways No 31323 and returned to duties on 10th February 1949.

In September 1949 and August 1953 it was again on loan to the National Coal Board at Snowdown Colliery. By May 1951 it was transferred to Dover shed, where it was to remain until withdrawn in the week ending 9th July 1960, having completed 564,623 miles in service.

No 31323 was sold to the Bluebell Railway, leaving Ashford for Brighton on Sunday 26th June 1960. It travelled forward from Brighton to Horsted Keynes the next day, becoming the second locomotive in the Bluebell Railway's fleet.

Above left: **The locomotive here carries the later variation of SR livery with 'shaded' lettering and numbers on the tank sides. This view was taken in 1948 following its last general overhaul by the Southern Railway at Ashford Works between November 1946 and January 1947.**
Steamchest collection

Left: **No 31323, in its first BR livery of unlined black, with the early style of BR totem, is seen at Ashford shed on 7th August 1952. It was returned to traffic in this livery on 19th June 1952 following its first BR general overhaul at Ashford Works.**
H C Casserley

No 31592

The C class 0-6-0 was a direct development of the London Chatham & Dover Railway's 1891 B2 class. In 1898 William Kirtley, Locomotive Superintendent of the LC&DR, authorised six improved B2 class 0-6-0s, but because of the merger with the South Eastern Railway these were never built. Robert Surtees from Long-hedge Works, was appointed Chief Draughts-man of the new South Eastern & Chatham Railway based at Ashford Works. He applied some of the work done at Longhedge on the upgraded B2s when assisting H S Wainwright, Locomotive and Carriage Superintendent of the new company, to produce an 0-6-0 goods engine design, initially referred to as class B3, but later redesignated as class C.

In all, 109 C class locomotives were con-structed between 1900 and 1908. Of these, two batches of 15 were built by outside contractors, 70 were built at Ashford and 9 at Longhedge, the latter being the last engines constructed there.

No 592 was the first of the batch constructed at Longhedge Works. Believed to have been completed in December 1901, she was handed over to the Running Department in February 1902. Painted in lined brunswick green livery No 592's first allocation was to Longhedge shed.

Top right: **From the Spring of 1916 the livery carried by class C locomotives was unlined grey. Following the Grouping in 1923 the class was repainted in black livery with narrow single lining in green. The number, prefixed with 'A', was applied to the sides of the tender. In this condition A592 is seen near Bromley in Kent, on 15th January 1932.** H C Casserley

Right: **The SR renumbered its fleet from 1931, dropping the letters prefixing the numbers. Renumbered 1592 during the course of an overhaul which ended on 17th March 1934, in its new guise the locomotive was recorded at New Cross Gate on 5th July 1934.** H N James

The C class was a sturdy and well-proportioned design. It remained the standard goods engine of the SE&CR until the Grouping in 1923 and the backbone of goods engine stock on the Southern Railway until Nationalisation. During the First World War they were associated with ammunition trains known as 'gunpowder specials'. In the Second World War they were involved with troop movements from the Channel ports following the Dunkirk evacuation in May and June 1940. Rare cine footage of these trains appears on Midland's *Vintage Southern* video.

From 1938 shaded sans-serif capital letters and numerals were introduced, with the number on the cabsides and the word 'Southern' on the tender. It is likely that No 1592 was treated in this way in December 1941. In late 1945 it was allocated to Ramsgate shed and appears to have remained there until June 1959. During this time it was renumbered 31592 by BR.

In June 1959 No 31592 was reallocated to Nine Elms shed, London. This was short-lived because in February 1960 it transferred to Tonbridge. A further transfer in November 1961 took it to Ashford shed.

No 31592 was loaned to Departmental Stock in June 1962, and a snowplough was fitted later that year. When heavy snows swept across Britain, Nos 31271 and 31592, coupled tender to tender, and with snowploughs fitted to their front buffer beams, were employed all over Kent. The snowplough was removed in the early Summer of 1963. Withdrawn from Capital Stock on Sunday 8th September 1963, together with the other two remaining class C locomotives Nos 31271 and 31280, on the following day all three left Ashford shed in steam, No 31592 being the last. They passed over the main line and went into Ashford Works yard. Almost immediately 31592 was renumbered DS239 in Departmental Stock, and used for shunting the yard. During the Summer of 1964 it was given an intermediate overhaul in Ashford Works.

DS239 remained in regular service until 1st October 1966, when steam operations at Ashford officially ceased. However its last duty was actually on Saturday 8th October 1966 when at 11.30 am its fire was dropped for the last time.

Top: **This view, probably taken in 1949, shows the locomotive in its early BR condition. Renumbered 31592, with the words British Railways on the side of the tender, the engine has also been fitted with a BR smoke box number plate.**
W M J Jackson, courtesy The Lyon collection

Above: **This view taken in the yard at Ramsgate shed on 28th June 1959 shows the locomotive carrying the first variety of BR totem and a 74B shedplate. Ramsgate shed was recoded from 74B to 73G with effect from 13th October 1958.**
Philip J Kelley

Above: **No 31592 and another C class at Stewarts Lane shed. Tender No 2885 was attached whilst on general overhaul in 1955 (ex-Works on 6th July 1955) and retained into preservation.** Lens of Sutton

Above: **No 31592 and another unidentified C class locomotive are seen trundling through Ashford Station in 1962. The former is carrying the second variety of BR totem, probably applied during its Works visit in February 1961.** David Lawrence

Below: **At Ashford shed on 18th November 1962, the last three C class locomotives that were to remain in traffic are seen together. No 31592 is coupled to No 31280, whilst No 31271 is to the right of the picture. All are in light steam.** Dave Idle

Above: **No 31592 is seen in the yard at Ashford shed on 18th August 1963.**
Dave Idle

Above: **During the heavy snows of the Winter of 1962-63, No 31592 (nearest the camera) coupled to No 31271, was recorded on snow-ploughing duties at New Romney on 1st January 1963.** G A Barlow,
courtesy of R F Stephens collection

Below: **In its final guise as DS239, our locomotive is seen shunting in the yard at Ashford Works in September 1963.** R F Stephens collection

The Wainwright C class Preservation Society formed in November 1962. At that time British Railways offered a C class for £1,100 in static condition, or £1,300 in working order. Four years later the purchase price had increased. Captain Peter Manisty of the Association of Railway Preservation Societies managed to negotiate a package deal with BR for the purchase of J36 class 0-6-0 No 65243 *Maude*, 1F 0-6-0 tank No 41708 and No 31592. The price for the latter had now gone up to £1,420; this was paid and the transaction was completed on 22nd December 1966.

In January 1967 the engine was positioned alongside the north east wall of the main erecting shops at Ashford Works, adjacent to the main line. By 10th March 1968 it had been moved to the former Ashford steam shed, which became the South Eastern Steam Centre.

Because of problems encountered there, it was decided to move No 31592 to the Bluebell Railway. The engine and tender were moved out of Ashford shed by rail, on the morning of 15th August 1970, through Ashford Station to the West yard, where the engine was winched onto a low-loader. The movement of both engine and tender to the Bluebell had been completed by 17th August where this sole survivor of a once numerous class continues to enjoy an active retirement.

No 31618

In the Spring of 1927 20 additional class K 2-6-4 tank locomotives had been authorised for construction. They were to be numbered A610 to A629 and named after rivers in the same series as A790 to A809. Due to the derailment of 2-6-4T A800 at Sevenoaks on 24th August 1927, they were not built. However the SR Running Department had been pressing for more 2-6-0 tender engines with 6ft driving wheels. It was decided therefore to build Nos A610 to A629 as tender engines, but due to adverse publicity given to the 'River' class by the national press it was decided that the new Moguls would not carry names. They were intended as replacements for old, small four-coupled passenger engines, and would be suitable for medium-weight passenger trains on sharply-graded routes where heavier 4-6-0s were prohibited.

A618 was constructed at Brighton Works in October 1928. Originally fitted with 3,500 gallon tender No 1908, its first allocation was to Guild-ford shed. It would have carried the name *River Hamble* had it been built as a 2-6-4T. Renumbered 1618 in the 1931 scheme, in that year its original chimney was replaced by one of the type used on the U1 class 2-6-0s. In common with other members of the class, No 1618 was fitted with smoke deflectors in 1935. In November 1938 it was paired at Ashford Works with a new 4,000 gallon tender No 3090, which had been built at Eastleigh. Its original tender was then fitted to the Q class 0-6-0 No 540.

During the Second World War it was often on passenger and freight trains, on the Reading branch; its livery was then unlined black. In February 1944 its tender was exchanged for one of 3,500 gallons capacity and in December 1945 it was reallocated to Salisbury shed.

The locomotive was renumbered 31618 by BR in mid-1948. Apparently it was viewed as something like the black sheep of its class. At Eastleigh shed on 9th July 1950 it was observed having the amount of coal going into its tender carefully weighed before the first of a planned series of trial runs on which its performance was to have been monitored by Eastern Region dynamometer car No 902532. However, these had to be abandoned when No 31618 ran hot and had to return to Eastleigh for repairs.

It was allocated to a variety of sheds throughout its BR career, including Nine Elms, Reading South, Dorchester, Guildford, Basingstoke and Eastleigh. For some of its time at the latter it was sub-shedded at Andover Junction. Its final home was Guildford to which it was allocated in March 1963.

No 31618's last general overhaul took place at Ashford Works from 7th to the 29th of March 1961. During the course of this it was fitted with a BR Standard class 4 chimney and blastpipe, and had the second variety of BR totem applied.

The locomotive was withdrawn from service on 12th January 1964, its final mileage being 1,143,942.

In its final SR livery, with its number on the cabsides, and attached to a 3,500 gallon tender, the loco was at Salisbury shed on 20th September 1947. H C Casserley

By 25th January 1964 it was in store in the open at Fratton shed. Sold for scrap to Woodham Brothers at Barry, it moved there under its own steam on 18th June 1964.

Saved for preservation, at a cost of £2,000 by the Southern Mogul Preservation Society it became only the second locomotive to leave the Barry scrapyard when, on 18th January 1969, it was hauled by the then Type 3, latterly class 37, No D6881, travelling via Reading to the Blackhorse sidings of Albert E Reed & Company Ltd, New Hythe, near Aylesford, in Kent.

Subsequently moved to the Kent & East Sussex Railway, where it was restored, it was taken by road from Tenterden to the Bluebell Railway in May 1977.

Right: **BR No 31618 speeds through Brockley hauling the 5.25 pm London Bridge-Reading on 22nd May 1952. Next to the tender is an ex-London & South Western Railway tri-composite carriage in red livery.**
C R L Coles, courtesy The Lyon collection

Below: **No 31618 pauses at Swindon Town on 28th September 1957, while working a Cheltenham to Southampton train on the former Midland & South Western Junction line. At this time a large proportion of through trains over this route were hauled by SR moguls.** D W Winkworth

No 31638

The earlier class U 2-6-0 locomotives proved so useful and popular on all sections of the Southern Railway that in 1930 ten more, numbered A630 to A639, were ordered. These machines were constructed at Ashford Works between February and May 1931. They were fitted with 4,000 gallon tenders from new, and differed from the rest of the class in having flat-topped domes.

No A638 was completed in May 1931, painted olive green, and allocated to Redhill, although shortly after it was moved to Guildford shed. Under the 1931 renumbering scheme it soon became No 1638. Before the Second World War it was fitted with smoke-deflectors and an U1-pattern chimney. During the War it was painted in unlined black and in 1943 it was transferred to Exmouth Junction.

In mid-November 1946 it arrived at Eastleigh earmarked for possible conversion to oil-burning though this did not take place.

In October 1948, whilst allocated to Nine Elms, it was repainted in BR lined black livery and renumbered 31638. Around May 1949 it exchanged tenders, receiving one holding 3,500 gallons, No 1950. In July 1949 it was transferred to Battersea shed, although on 27th August 1949 it was observed at work on the Barnstaple-Ilfracombe line. No 31638 was subject to many transfers in its BR days. During October 1949 it was allocated to Faversham; by May 1951 it was at Hither Green, in July 1951 at Redhill, in September 1951 it moved to Brighton, and in October of that year to Eastleigh. During April 1952 it was tried out on trains between Cheltenham Lansdown and Andover Junction on the former Midland & South Western Junction route, in place of WR 2-6-0s. More transfers occurred in 1953: in January to Redhill shed, in June to Hither Green, and in September to Fratton.

During a general overhaul at Ashford Works in October 1955 it was paired with another 3,500 gallon tender, No 3028. At its last general overhaul at Ashford Works in July 1959, Automatic Train Control gear was fitted.

With the commencement of the Winter timetable on 2nd November 1959, Fratton shed closed. Its final allocation of 23 locomotives, included seven 'Terriers' and No 31638. Upon closure No 31638 was reallocated for the last time, going to Guildford, and returned to working Redhill-Reading trains as it had done in the 1930s.

Withdrawn from service on 12th January 1964, by the 25th of that month it was back at Fratton lying out of use. Sold for scrap to Woodham Brothers, Barry, it was towed there by No 31618 on 18th June 1964.

No 31638 was the last former Southern Railway U class locomotive to remain at Barry and was the 114th locomotive to be purchased for preservation. It arrived on the Bluebell to join No 31618 on 1st August 1980.

A638, with its original 4,000 gallon tender, leaves Guildford on 21st May 1932.
H C Casserley

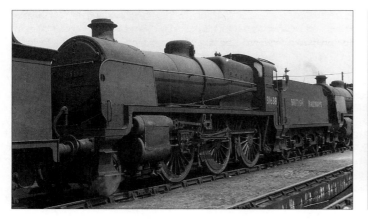

Above: **No 31638, in its first BR post-1948 livery, is sporting the name of new owner 'British Railways' on its tender.** Lens of Sutton

Above: **With a train of Bulleid stock, No 31638 is awaiting departure from Southampton Central on 20th January 1956.** H C Casserley

Below: **Carrying a Guildford (70C) shedplate, No 31638 is at Ashford awaiting a heavy intermediate overhaul in February 1962.**
B Webb collection, courtesy Industrial Railway Society

No 32473

Between 1891 and 1905 R J Billinton was responsible for 134 six-coupled tanks being built, consisting of three types divided into four classes, known as E3, E4, E5 and E6. Following the E3 class, designed for shorter distance goods services, the next order of 0-6-2 tanks had the diameter of their coupled wheels increased by 6 inches to 5 ft, for working secondary passenger, suburban, and mixed traffic services. They were known as Radial Tanks because of the radial axles on their trailing trucks. A radial axle does not just carry weight from the main frames directly or via a conventional pony truck, it is an axle in which the axle-boxes are housed, and the axle assembly itself moves, in radial guides. The sideways movement is able to accommodate bends more easily.

The first 12 were ordered in March 1896 and were known as the class E Specials. From 1904 when D E Marsh took office they were re-classified as E4s. This batch was numbered from 463 to 474, and was built at Brighton Works between December 1897 and August 1898 at a cost of £26,640, an average of £2,220 each. No 473 was the eleventh member of the class to be built, completed in June 1898 and allocated to New Cross shed.

It was originally named *Birch Grove*, retaining the name until 1912. This was one of 588 names given to LB&SCR locomotives. The E4 class were mostly named after towns and villages within the area served by the company, however *Birch Grove* was named after a country house near to Horsted Keynes, on the present Bluebell Railway, the family home of the Macmillan publishing dynasty, whose most notable scion, Harold Macmillan later the Earl of Stockton, was a director of the GWR in the 1930s, and Prime Minister from January 1957 to October 1963. His place of burial is at Horsted Keynes.

From August 1912 the original R J Billinton pattern boilers were replaced on the E4 class by boilers with an extended smokebox, designed by Colonel L B Billinton. No 473 was modified in this way in September 1912, receiving boiler No 891 which it retained until July 1920. This boiler, No 891, was again fitted when it had its last BR general overhaul at Ashford Works in 1960 and is the boiler it carried into preservation.

By 1923 No 473 was allocated to Brighton shed. In February 1924 it was repainted in SR lined green and renumbered B473. Following an overhaul at Ashford Works which was concluded on 23rd December 1932, the locomotive was renumbered 2473.

***Birch Grove*, in Stroudley livery, in company with a class C2 0-6-0 goods engine, at its home shed of New Cross about 1904.**
RAS Marketing

In July 1945 No 2473 was recorded as being allocated to Norwood Junction shed. Early in 1948 it was one of seven of the class to be renumbered with an 's' prefix, becoming British Railways s2473. During a visit to Ashford Works for overhaul in April 1951, it was renumbered 32473. In September 1950 it was transferred to Bricklayers Arms shed where it later spent nine months in store from September 1955 to May 1956.

Several members of the class were reallocated in 1955 to Western Section sheds such as Nine Elms, Eastleigh, Salisbury, Dorchester, Reading, and Guildford. The turn of No 32473 came in June 1960 when it was transferred to what became its final shed, Nine Elms, where it was used for working empty coaching stock trains between Clapham Junction carriage sidings and Waterloo station.

The only member of the E4 class taken out of service before Nationalisation was No 2483 in October 1944. Most of the class were withdrawn between 1955 and 1963, their final year in service. No 32473's turn came on 27th October 1962; its final mileage a remarkable 1,203,967. Only six locomotives of the class remained in service after No 32473's withdrawal, the last of these going in June 1963.

Purchased for preservation, in October 1962, on the 16th of that month it worked light engine from Nine Elms shed to Horsted Keynes to begin its honourable and well earned active retirement on the Bluebell Railway.

Above left: **In company with a number of other ex-LB&SCR Radial tanks, including sister engine No 2467, our loco is seen at Norwood Junction shed on 28th July 1945.**
H C Casserley

Left: **The first variety of BR totem was applied during its works visit in March 1951. That style of totem was still being carried when the engine was photographed at Bricklayers Arms shed on 19th April 1959. At its general overhaul in May 1960, the second type of BR totem was applied.**
L Hanson

No 32636

William Stroudley was appointed the Locomotive Superintendent of the London Brighton & South Coast Railway on 1st February 1870. The class A 0-6-0 tank was his design for a fleet of powerful, yet lightly constructed engines to handle suburban working in the London area.

No 72 *Fenchurch* was one of the first of the class to be built at Brighton Works, Nos 70 to 75 being constructed there between September and December 1872. No 71 was the first completed, and along with No 72 it left the erecting shop on 28th August 1872. No 72 however was the first to be put into service, on 7th September 1872. Built at a cost of £1,800, No 72's first allocation was to Battersea shed.

In 1898 having covered 599,297 miles for the LB&SCR, it was sold to the Newhaven Harbour Company for £350. It had arrived at Newhaven by 27th June, still retaining its Stroudley livery and name but not its numberplates or Westinghouse brake. In 1904, when it was repaired at Brighton Works, 14 inch cylinders were fitted, making it the most powerful engine of the class.

It was outshopped in February of that year in green livery. On a further visit to Brighton Works in April 1913 it was re-boilered with a Marsh designed boiler and reclassified A1X, all at a cost of £1,195. It was turned out in black livery with red lining and lettered 'Newhaven Harbour Company', on the tank sides.

When the Newhaven Harbour Company was acquired by the Southern Railway in 1926, this locomotive, with a book value of £575, was included in the sale. It entered Brighton Works in December 1926, was repainted in unlined black, renumbered as SR B636, leaving the works in January 1927 to go back to Newhaven. It was to remain allocated to Newhaven until 1955, by which time it would have been there for 57 years.

Under the SR 1931 renumbering scheme it became No 2636. However the locomotive did not carry this number until January 1936 when it was applied using some former LB&SCR gilt numerals against a background of a plain unlined black livery.

During a visit to Brighton Works in June 1950 it was repainted in lined black, renumbered as British Railways 32636 and was given the first variety of BR totem.

In preparation for working special trips to Kemp Town in connection with the Brighton Works centenary specials in October 1952, No 32636 was given trials on passenger trains, using a Brighton motor set, between Eastbourne and Hailsham from 28th July to 1st August 1952. The Railway Correspondence and Travel Society ran special trains between Victoria and Brighton on the 5th and 19th of October 1952 in connection with the centenary. No 32636, then the oldest surviving engine on the Southern Region, ran three trips each day between Brighton and Kemp Town. The train was an ex-LB&SCR two coach push-pull set No 727 specially brought over from Gillingham.

In this photograph taken at Battersea shed, *Fenchurch* displays the Westinghouse brake pump with which it had been fitted in 1878. The locomotive is still in its original Stroudley livery and has condensing pipes for working through the Thames tunnel.
L G Marshall collection

Above: **Following repairs at Brighton Works in 1910 the locomotive was repainted in lined black livery. Still bearing its LB&SCR name painted in yellow, it is seen on its new owner's premises at East Quay shed at Newhaven.** L G Marshall collection

Above: **On a further visit to Brighton Works in October 1922 it was again repainted, its owner's name being applied to the tank sides. In this photograph the locomotive is outside Newhaven Town shed, probably in 1926. The original lettering is just visible beneath the present lettering on the tank sides.** R C Stumpf collection

No 32636 was stored at Newhaven for six weeks during the winter of 1953/54, and again from June 1955 for two months during the national railway strike. In October 1955 it was transferred to St Leonards shed for use on the former Kent & East Sussex line.

By April 1958 it was hailed as the oldest engine in service on British Railways and the oldest surviving Brighton built locomotive. About this time it acquired the second style of BR totem.

Opposite page bottom: **No 2636 and sister loco No 2647 are seen together at Newhaven shed in 1947. No 2647 was withdrawn from service in October 1951 without acquiring its BR identity.** Steamchest collection

Below: **No 32636 is engaged on shed pilot duties at St Leonards in mid-1958. In the background are two 'Schools' class 4-4-0s, of which only No 30935** Sevenoaks **can be identified.** David Lawrence

On 2nd June 1958 it worked the last steam hauled goods to Tenterden on the former K&ESR line, after which a class 04 diesel took over this duty. No 32636 left St Leonards shed on 5th September 1959. It was at Eastbourne shed from 7th September to 11th October 1959; thereafter it was based at Fratton to work the Hayling Island branch. In early 1960, reallocated to Brighton shed, it was back at Newhaven Harbour again. In March 1961 it was working at Lancing Carriage Works.

At Newhaven on 14th February 1962 No 32636 was involved in an accident. Fortunately it was sent to Eastleigh Works where a decision was made to give it what was to be its last BR general repair. By the time this had been completed in May 1962 No 32636 had been given a new firebox, repainted in lined black livery and new-style condensed numerals of the variety then being applied to diesel locomotives.

During the first half of 1963 it was working again at Lancing Carriage Works, eventually departing from there on 13th June 1963. It was back at Fratton in September 1963 for use on the Hayling Island branch. On 3rd November 1963 the Locomotive Club of Great Britain ran 'The Hayling Farewell Rail Tour', which was worked by No 32636 and sister engine No 32670 to mark the closure of the branch the following day.

No 32636 was withdrawn from service on 4th November 1963 with a total recorded mileage of 1,109,513. It was stored at Fratton shed until 4th January 1964 when it was towed by No 32662 to Eastleigh.

Bought by the Bluebell Railway for £750, it left Eastleigh under its own steam on 11th May 1964 for Brighton shed. It arrived on the Bluebell Railway on 13th May to enter the next phase of its long career.

No 32655

No 55 *Stepney* was another of the 50 A class tanks designed by William Stroudley, for light passenger traffic, particularly on the South London lines of the London, Brighton & South Coast Railway. Ten still survive in preservation.

LB&SCR No 55 was one of the third batch (Nos 52 to 63) built at Brighton Works in 1875-76. The average cost of construction of this batch was £1,875. No 55 entered service on 21st December 1875, at New Cross shed. Details of its early life are sketchy but it was shedded at

New Cross in April 1887, the middle of the 1890s and in 1902. The locomotive was renumbered 655 on the Duplicate List in June 1901 and transferred to Brighton in 1902.

By March 1912 it was on allocation to West Croydon shed. In October of that year it was rebuilt as a Class A1X, being fitted with one of 12 new boilers built at Brighton works in 1911-12. The cost of reboilering was £865. At this time, the locomotive had accumulated a mileage of 750,043.

No 655 was loaned in 1920 to the Woolmer Instructional Military Railway, forerunner of the Longmoor Military Railway and by 31st Decem-

ber 1922, just prior to the Grouping, it had completed 926,064 miles and was allocated to Portsmouth shed.

In 1925 it was withdrawn from traffic and stored in Preston Park paint shop at Brighton. Reinstated in January 1927, it was fitted with a new boiler (which it retained until November

Seen at Brighton Station about 1906, the locomotive is in gamboge livery with gold leaf transfers and has wooden brake blocks. The train consists of non-corridor 4-wheel Billinton stock. R C Stumpf collection

1939), vacuum brakes and London & South Western Railway designed mechanical push-pull gear. Repainted in SR green livery and numbered B655, the loco was transferred to Fratton to work the Lee-on-Solent branch.

By 1936 it had been renumbered 2655 and continued to work from Fratton shed, mainly on the Hayling Island branch, until 1938, when it was hired to the Kent & East Sussex Railway. Based at Rolvenden, it was used on hop-picking traffic until these workings ceased in October 1939.

No 2655 emerged from Eastleigh Works on 21st December 1939 repainted in unlined dark green with new style lettering. By January 1942 it was in store at Fratton shed. At Brighton Works in November 1945 the locomotive was given a very heavy overhaul which was practically a re-build.

Renumbered by British Railways to 32655 in late December 1949 at Brighton works, at this time the loco was painted lined black and given the first variety of BR totem. By 1953 it had returned to working on the former Kent & East Sussex line, being based at St Leonards.

In late October 1955 it was reallocated to Brighton, though it was normally sub-shedded at Newhaven where it shunted at the harbour. Its long career ended when it was withdrawn from service in the week ending 28th May 1960 with a final mileage of 1,396,027.

It was sold for £550 to the Bluebell Railway and delivered on 17th May 1960, becoming the first locomotive in the railway's collection.

Above right: In its last Southern Railway livery of wartime black, numbered 2655, the locomotive is at Havant on a Hayling Island train in 1947. It was still working on this branch two years later. Steamchest collection

Right: No 32655 is seen here on a Tenterden Town to Robertsbridge train at Tenterden Town on 3rd August 1955. The coach is an ex-L&SWR bogie corridor brake third. D W Winkworth

No 33001

At the beginning of the Second World War the Southern Railway had a surplus of motive power because of wartime reductions in passenger services. However Bulleid realised that in time there could be a shortage of locomotives to handle the greatly increased freight traffic which the SR was having to cope with. On Bulleid's recommendation in August 1940, the SR Board authorised the construction of 40 powerful freight engines.

Bulleid decided on a completely new concept incorporating the largest possible boiler and firebox with all unnecessary frills cut out, to attain maximum power with minimum weight, and produce a locomotive far superior to the Q class 0-6-0 introduced in 1938. The 40 locomotives of the Q1 class were built between March and December 1942; 20 each were constructed at Brighton and Ashford Works. They were originally to have been numbered 550 to 589, following on from the number sequence of Maunsell's Q class 0-6-0s, however Bulleid decided to use his own variation of the Continental system in which the letter C denoted a six-coupled wheel arrangement.

On 6th May 1942 No C1 was inspected by the directors of the Southern Railway and the press at Charing Cross Station in London.

In September 1942 it was on test freight trips between Norwood in South London, and Chichester. In December 1942 Nos C1 and C3 were tested against S15 class 4-6-0 No 842 in a series of trials with 65-wagon goods trains, between Woking and Basingstoke.

Left: C1 was completed at Brighton Works in March 1942 at a cost of £9,115. This official Southern Railway photograph is dated 26th March 1942. R C Stumpf collection

Below: C1 is seen on a ballast train at Redhill on 16th August 1947.
LCGB / Ken Nunn collection

In service there appeared few limits to the haulage capability or route availability of the Q1 class. Following Nationalisation, C1 was renumbered 33001 on 13th November 1950.

Its last general overhaul lasted from 19th January to 14th February 1955 at Ashford Works. In June 1959 it was allocated to Tonbridge shed, in February 1961 to Feltham and in September 1963 it had moved to Guildford.

In January 1964 No 33001 was placed in store at Nine Elms shed. It was withdrawn from service on 17th May 1964 with a final mileage of 459,057. Final mileages for the Q1 class ranged between 450,000 and 500,000. Following withdrawal, it was set aside for preservation in the National Collection. It was kept at first at Nine Elms shed, then moved to the paint shop at Stratford works in East London, and later to the former Pullman Works at Preston Park just outside Brighton.

It was given on long term loan to the Bluebell and was moved by road from Brighton via Haywards Heath to the railway, being delivered there on 15th May 1977.

Below: **BR No 33001 on a passenger train duty when allocated to Feltham shed. The locomotive is seen at Bramley & Wonersh Station, hauling a Guildford to Cranleigh train in 1961.** Mike Esau

No 34023 *Blackmore Vale*

When O V S Bulleid was appointed Chief Mechanical Engineer of the Southern Railway in 1937, many of its non-electrified services were being handled by elderly locomotives. There was a need to modernise the steam fleet and the 'West Country' light Pacific was one of Bulleid's notable designs produced for this end. Similar to, but lighter than the earlier 'Merchant Navy' class, the 'West Country' Pacifics had a much wider route availability.

Just two months old, No 21C123 is on the turntable at Stewarts Lane shed on 13th April 1946.
Pursey Short, courtesy Mike Esau

No 21C123 was built at Brighton works to order number 2561, dated 28th September 1944. The average cost of building the first 30 'West Country' Pacifics was £17,060. Completed in February 1946, fitted with boiler No 1279 and paired with 4,500 gallon tender No 3273, the locomotive was turned out in the SR's malachite green livery.

Its first allocation was to Ramsgate shed. As a South Eastern Division loco, it went to Ashford Works for attention. It visited the works no less than four times in 1946, and again in April 1947, a reflection perhaps of some of the problems associated with the many innovations introduced by Bulleid in his Pacific designs. In June 1947 it was transferred to Nine Elms Shed, in London. The Pacific did not receive its name, *Blackmoor Vale,* until August of that year. In April 1948 it was renumbered by British Railways as 34023.

The locomotive takes its name from a part of Dorset. Seventeenth century maps described this as the Vale of Blakemore, modern atlases call the area Blackmoor Vale. This was the spelling on the original plates fitted by the SR,

but British Railways decided that Blackmore Vale was the correct form and the new plates were duly made and fitted in April 1950.

Reallocated to Salisbury shed, in November 1950 it spent about a month in store there. With apparently little work for it to do at Salisbury, it was transferred to Nine Elms shed, where it was soon back in store. It was reallocated to Exmouth Junction shed to work services on the SR lines west of Exeter in May 1951.

Early in 1957 No 34023 was observed hauling through trains between Exeter and Brighton. During a light intermediate overhaul at Eastleigh works in April 1960 it was fitted with AWS gear.

On 28th September 1963, Exmouth Junction shed, where No 34023 was still allocated, passed from the control of the Southern Region to the Western Region, being recoded from 72A to 83D. At the end of September 1964 No 34023 was transferred back to the Southern Region, to Eastleigh shed.

In May 1967 it returned again to Nine Elms shed where it saw out the end of steam workings on the Southern Region on Sunday 9th July 1967 having completed 921,268 miles.

Purchased for preservation at a cost of £1,900 by the Bulleid Pacific Preservation Society, it was moved by rail to the Longmoor Military Railway, where it was kept at first.

In September 1971 it was transferred to what has become its permanent home on the Bluebell railway.

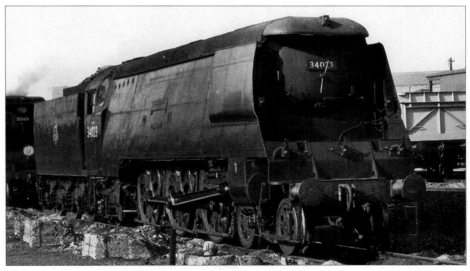

Top left: **No 34023 has been entrusted to haul the prestigious 'Atlantic Coast Express'. It is still in malachite green, with the Southern Railway plate on the smokebox door and its original *Blackmoor Vale* nameplates, but it carries its new number and 'British Railways' name on the tender.** R L Inns collection

Top right: **At Exmouth Junction shed in May 1952, No 34023 is carrying the first style of BR totem and replacement nameplates.**
R L Inns collection

Above: **During a heavy intermediate overhaul at Eastleigh Works in October 1954, the locomotive's cab was modified to a 'V' shape as can be seen by comparing this picture with the others on this page. This photograph must have been taken before May 1957 when the locomotive behind it, No 35008, was rebuilt. The forward valancing in front of the cylinders has also been removed from No 34023.**
R L Inns collection

Right: **By mid-June 1966 No 34023's nameplates had been removed. In this state it is illustrated here hauling the 'Dorset Coast Express' at Corfe Castle, on the Swanage branch, on 7th May 1967.** A Swain

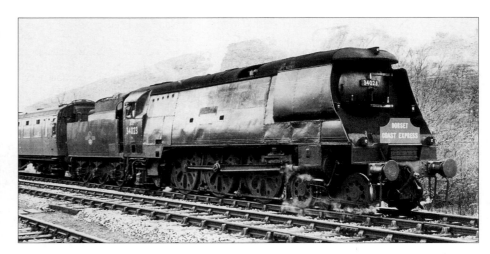

Below: **No 34023 *Blackmore Vale* is seen here at Basingstoke. Its tender, No 311, has been modified by reducing the height of the tender's sides. This work was carried out during the course of an overhaul which was completed on 10th February 1962. This photograph is believed to have been taken, around September 1963.** Lens of Sutton

No 34059 *Sir Archibald Sinclair*

Bulleid's light Pacific design for the Southern Railway was divided into two classes, the 'Battle of Britain' and 'West Country' which were distinguished by their names rather than detailed design differences.

One hundred and ten engines were constructed between May 1945 and January 1951; 104 at Brighton and the other six at Eastleigh. As built, the Pacifics incorporated a host of unconventional features ranging from Bulleid's distinctive system of numbering and streamlined casing to valve gear enclosed in an oil bath which was prone to leaking. Sixty of the class, including this locomotive, were subsequently rebuilt, losing their streamlined casing and being equipped with Walschaerts valve gear in the process.

No 21C159 was built at Brighton Works to Order No 3213 for 25 locomotives, Nos 21C146 to 21C170, inclusive. The average cost per engine of this order was £20,220. Its frames had been laid by 19th December 1946 and it was completed in April 1947. As built it was fitted with boiler No 1313, 4,500 gallon tender No 3310 and was painted in malachite green livery.

Allocated to Nine Elms shed in London, it was soon working services to Southampton, Salisbury, and Bournemouth. On 16th May 1947 it was observed heading the down 'Atlantic Coast Express'. It was the first light Pacific to work from Southampton Docks, on an up Jersey boat train on 5th July 1947. On 16th July 1947 it hauled the 'Bournemouth Belle' from Waterloo.

The Pacific visited Brighton Works in December 1947, during which time its cab was modified and the nameplates *Sir Archibald Sinclair* and a plaque were attached. The nameplates were covered over until the official naming ceremony on 24th February 1948 at Waterloo Station. The ceremony was carried out by the Rt Hon Sir Archibald Sinclair, Bart, KT, CMG, MP, leader of the Liberal Party in the British House of Commons from 1935, and Secretary of State for Air from 11th May 1940 until 28th May 1945 when he was succeeded by the Rt Hon Harold Macmillan, MP.

Following Nationalisation it was renumbered BR s21C159 at Ashford on 21st February 1948, and renumbered again to 34059 at Eastleigh on 11th March 1949, BR dropping Bulleid's numbering system. At this time the locomotive was paired with 4,500 gallon tender No 3289. The locomotive was exhibited during the Waterloo Centenary Exhibition held at Waterloo Station from 14th to 25th June 1948.

In early 1949 it was perceived within BR that the Southern Region possessed many more light Pacifics than it needed. To explore the feasibility of moving 15 to the Eastern Region, No 34059 was transferred on loan to Stratford shed on 27th April 1949. There it worked trains from Liverpool Street to Norwich, Yarmouth, Parkeston Quay, and Cambridge. However the idea was not pursued, and by 30th May 1949 it was back at Nine Elms shed.

No 34059 blotted its copybook on 26th August 1950 when it failed whilst working the up 'Bournemouth Belle', requiring substitution by 'King Arthur' class 4-6-0 No 30780 to complete the journey. Repainted in BR brunswick green in April 1951, it was transferred the same month to Exmouth Junction shed. No 34059 began making appearances working through Newton

Abbot on some of the SR turns along the former GWR main lines between Plymouth and Exeter. These workings ensured the SR crews had route knowledge of these tracks, useful if there were disruptions or adverse weather conditions on their own line between these two locations. The locomotive was also recorded in charge of the 'Devon Belle' at this period. A change of tenders took place at Exmouth Junction shed in September 1954, with No 34059 receiving 4,500 gallon tender No 3273 from sister engine No 34023, later to be a stablemate on the Bluebell Railway (see pages 56 to 58).

By September 1955 it had been re allocated to Salisbury whilst in the early part of 1957 it was recorded working on through trains between Exeter and Brighton.

In 1960 No 34059 was the first of 15 locomotives to be rebuilt to Order No H09886, and as a result became the 31st light Pacific to be rebuilt.

21C159 is seen at Southampton Central in 1947. Note the SR lettering and numerals, also the clean lines of its original tender, No 3310. C Banks collection

Photographs on the opposite page:

Top left: During its brief sojourn on the Eastern Region No 34059 was recorded at Norwich Thorpe shed on 18th May 1949 prior to working 'The Norfolkman' to London Liverpool Street. LCGB / Ken Nunn collection

Top right: An interesting line-up of locomotives at Norwich Thorpe shed on 18th May 1949. With No 34059 are D16/3 class 4-4-0 No 62535 and B1 class 4-6-0 No 1270. LCGB / Ken Nunn collection

Bottom: No 34059 in rebuilt form, on a stopping train to Exeter, at Basingstoke in the early 1960s. R L Inns collection

The average cost of rebuilding this batch was £12,864. It emerged from Eastleigh in the week ending 26th March 1960. From 1960 the rebuilt No 34059 was allocated to Salisbury shed. Its last major overhaul was a heavy intermediate repair which was undertaken at Eastleigh Works between 25th October and 6th December 1963. The locomotive was withdrawn from service in the week ending 29th May 1966 by which time its recorded mileage was 877,107.

No 34059 was then sold for scrap to Woodham Brothers at Barry, where it arrived on 1st November 1966. By coincidence standard class 5 4-6-0 No 73082 which it later joined on the Bluebell Railway (see page 67), also arrived there that day.

It was purchased for preservation, without a tender, by the Bluebell Railway 'Battle of Britain' Locomotive Group which raised the £7,250 required in ten months. It was the 108th locomotive to leave Barry; again coincidentally the previous departure had been No 73082. The Pacific's departure marked the half way point in the Barry saga, with 107 locomotives remaining in the scrapyard.

No 34059 left Barry on 25th October 1979 and arrived on the Bluebell three days later.

Below: Seen here with only nine months active service left, No 34059 awaits departure time at Waterloo Station on 27th August 1965. John Edgington

No 35027 *Port Line*

Thirty locomotives of the 'Merchant Navy' class were built between 1941 and 1949. Bulleid's first 4-6-2 design incorporated many features new to British locomotive practice, ranging from a distinctive streamlined appearance on the outside to their chain driven valve gear on the inside.

No 35027 was built at Eastleigh Works as part of Order No 3393, for locomotives Nos 35021 to 35030, ordered at an estimated cost of £25,000 each. The tenders for this batch were built at Brighton. The final average cost for these locomotives was £31,348. No 35027 entered traffic on 11th December 1948, equipped with boiler No 1117 (built at a cost of £4,220) and 4,500 gallon tender No 3288, which had previously run with light Pacific No 21C135 *Shaftesbury*. Its initial livery was unlined malachite green. Lining was not applied because it had not yet been paired with its matching 6,000 gallon tender then under construction at Brighton.

Its first allocation was Bournemouth, where it was run-in on stopping trains to Weymouth and semi-fasts to Waterloo. It returned to Eastleigh in April 1949 where it was finally united with its 6,000 gallon tender No 3349.

In April 1950 it was reallocated to Stewarts Lane shed in London, where, with others in the 35025 to 35030 batch, it was employed on boat trains to Dover and Folkestone. These trains had been increasing in weight due to the post-war travel boom. In April 1950 it was repainted in blue livery and its official naming ceremony took place at Southampton Docks on 24th of that month, the nameplates being unveiled by Mr W Donald, Chairman of Port Line.

On 12th May 1953 No 35027 was temporarily withdrawn from traffic at Ashford due to suspect driving axles. Dismantled at Ashford, the axles were despatched by road to Eastleigh Works where they were tested by ultrasonic equipment. The locomotive returned to traffic on 17th May 1953 and in November of that year it was repainted in BR green livery during a light intermediate overhaul at Eastleigh Works. In October and November 1954 it was back at Eastleigh for its first general overhaul. At that time it was fitted with a modified, balanced pattern of crank axle and replacement boiler No 1098, set at a lower working pressure. In June 1955 it was trans-ferred back to Bournemouth shed where it was to remain until withdrawal.

It entered Eastleigh Works on 28th March 1957. Order No HO7998 called for 15 locomotives to be put through the works and rebuilt between February 1956 and May 1957, at an average estimated cost of £7,417.

No 35027 was the 14th of this order to be dealt with. It left the works in the week ending 4th May 1957 fitted with boiler No 1101, a new left-hand cylinder and with its tender also modified.

On 29th April 1959 the Queen and the Prince of Wales inspected HMS *Eagle* off Weymouth. On the previous evening No 35027 hauled the Royal Train from Windsor & Eton Riverside to the Hamworthy goods line, near Poole, where the train was berthed overnight. It also hauled the return train from Southampton.

During the course of its last general overhaul at Eastleigh Works from 9th August 1963 to 5th October 1963 it was fitted with boiler No 1115. Withdrawn from service in the week ending 18th September 1966 with a final mileage of 872,290, it was stored at Eastleigh before being sold to Woodham Brothers, Barry, for scrap. It arrived there in March 1967 and was one of ten 'Merchant Navy' Pacifics, one third of the class, to be sold to Woodhams.

Purchased in January 1982 by the Port Line Locomotive Project at a cost of £6,500, No 35027 was the 142nd engine to leave Barry. On 18th December 1982 it went to Blunsdon, on the Swindon & Cricklade Railway. When No 35027 left Barry it was paired with 5,000 gallon tender No 3116. This tender, from No 35006, had spent its entire life with that locomotive. Restoration was completed in the works weigh-house at Swindon. It was the first 'Merchant Navy' from Barry scrapyard to be steamed in preservation.

Following its appearance at the 'Woking 150' event, it was moved to the Bluebell Railway on 31st May 1988. Its inaugural run on the railway took place on 18th June.

Left: **No 35027 is seen here at Bournemouth Central on 25th June 1949, with no BR insignia on its 6,000 gallon tender, and with its nameplates covered.** R L Inns collection

Right: **After its return to Bournemouth in June 1955, No 35027 *Port Line* is seen working the down 'Bournemouth Belle' near Farnborough.** Bob Barnard

Below: **No 35027 had the honour of hauling, what was perhaps the Southern Region's most prestigious train, 'The Golden Arrow', on Sunday 20th May 1951. It is seen here arriving at Dover Marine station with the train.** Pursey Short, courtesy Mike Esau

Left: **'The Pines Express' was routed away from the Somerset & Dorset Joint line from 1963. No 35027 was often observed hauling this train on its new route between Bournemouth and Oxford. This photograph, taken before 14th October 1963, shows the Pacific at Oxford after such a working. A Western Region 22xx 0-6-0 may be glimpsed in the background.** R L Inns collection

Below: **Four months after rebuilding, No 35027 prepares to leave Bournemouth Central with the 11.10am to Waterloo on 21st September 1957.** D W Winkworth

No 58850

The North London Railway was incorporated as the East and West India Docks & Birmingham Junction Railway on 26th August 1846, and adopted its more familiar title in 1853. Whilst the London & North Western Railway had been working the line from 1st January 1909, the NLR survived formal absorption by the L&NWR until 1st January 1922.

William Adams was the NLR's first Locomotive Superintendent, appointed in 1854. He was responsible for establishing a works at Bow Junction and from 1863 the NLR was self-sufficient in manufacturing locomotives and rolling stock. The works at Bow built two types of 4-4-0 passenger tank locomotive; machines with inside cylinders from 1865, and those with outside cylinders after 1868. From 1873 J C Park succeeded Adams, and in July 1879 he introduced a class of 0-6-0Ts for goods and shunting duties. Thirty of these locomotives, subsequently known as the '75' class, were built.

Below left: **As LMS No 7505, the former NLR tank is seen at its long-time base, Devons Road shed in Bow, in the late 1920s. In 1958 this was the first BR shed to eliminate steam traction, operating diesels until closure in February 1964.** Steamchest collection

Below right: **Renumbered 27505 in June 1934, it is seen shunting at the foot of the 1 in 9 incline at Cromford in 1944.** P Coxon

Bottom left: **When it received its new BR number, 58850, in 1949, the legend 'British Railways' was placed on the tank sides above the number. The locomotive is seen fairly soon after renumbering, at the shed at Sheep Pasture on the C&HP section.** Steamchest collection

Bottom right: **Following its overhaul at Derby in 1961, the 0-6-0T was painted in unlined black and fitted with a cast iron 2650 numberplate, in the L&NWR style.** Steamchest collection

The NLR Locomotive, Stores and Traffic Committee Minute No 3939, dated 3rd February 1880, records the decision to build five more shunting engines at a cost of £1,650 each. These were Nos 76 to 80 inclusive, and the first of these, No 76, the eventual Bluebell locomotive, was completed in January 1882, as Bow Works No 181. Its original livery was lined green and it was at first fitted with a stovepipe chimney.

In 1883 the NLR had a stock of 80 locomotives, 63 of which were required for service on a given day. Approval was given in June 1885 to adopt black as the standard colour for engines, the reasons given were that it was more durable and easier to keep clean. Accordingly No 76 was so repainted. It was renumbered to 116 on the Duplicate List in October 1891 and rebuilt at Bow Works during October 1897, being allotted a new works number, 264. When taken into L&NWR stock, it was renumbered 2650 in August 1909. Following the Grouping of the railways in 1923, it became London Midland & Scottish Railway No 7505 from December 1926.

The first of the '75' class were moved in 1931 from London to Derbyshire to work on the Cromford & High Peak mineral line, where this locomotive was to remain until withdrawal by British Railways. The non-standard locomotives of the LM&SR were renumbered in the mid-1930s by adding 20,000 to the existing numbers, thus No 7505 became 27505 in June 1934.

Fifteen of the class passed into BR ownership. No 27505 assumed its new BR number, 58850, in the week ending 21st May 1949. It was withdrawn in September 1960, subsequently moving to Derby Works. It was fortunately purchased for preservation, the only NLR locomotive to survive.

Following an overhaul at Derby Works in the Autumn of 1961, it was moved to the Bluebell Railway, arriving there on 28th March 1962.

Above: **No 58850 at Derby in 1955 now carries a Rowsley, 17D, shedplate. It is worth noting that neither the LMS or BR saw fit to provide a smokebox door numberplate for the locomotive.** Steamchest collection

Below: **No 58850 waits with a train of open wagons and brake vans being used on this occasion for an Ian Allan Club Special, at Middleton Top on 25th September 1955.** John Edgington

Opposite page: **The newly completed No 73082 seen at Derby works on 27th June 1955, three days after it had officially entered traffic. The locomotive is turned out in BR's lined black livery.** R J Buckley

No 73082 *Camelot*

British Railways' Standard class 5 mixed traffic 4-6-0s were essentially a development of Sir William Stanier's design, dating from 1934, for the London, Midland & Scottish Railway, 842 of which were eventually built.

172 BR Standard class 5 locomotives were constructed between 1951 and 1957, 42 at Doncaster and the remainder at Derby. No 73082 was built to BR Lot No 241, at Derby Works in 1955, one of a batch of 15 locomotives numbered 73075 to 73089. Cost of construction of the engine and tender was £21,750. Allocated new to Stewarts Lane shed in London, No 73082 and her sisters were put to work on services to the Kent coast.

As the electrification of the Kent Coast lines neared completion No 73082 was transferred in June 1959 to Nine Elms, on the Western Section. In early 1959 it was decided that the Southern Region class 5s, Nos 73080 to 73089 and 73110 to 73119, were to receive the names previously carried by the N15 'King Arthur' class 4-6-0s, Nos 30736 to 30755. New nameplates were cast for the Standards. No 73082 received a light intermediate overhaul at Eastleigh Works between 28th July and 15th August 1959, during which time ATC apparatus was fitted. The locomotive emerged bearing the name *Camelot*, which had previously been carried by No 30742 and had been withdrawn in February 1957.

During the next six years it worked mainly on semi-fast trains from Waterloo to Salisbury, Southampton and Bournemouth. In May 1965 five Q1 0-6-0s were transferred from Guildford to Nine Elms in exchange for the same number of Standard class 5 4-6-0s, including No 73082.

Thereafter it regularly worked stopping trains on the Reading to Redhill line. During December 1965 it worked a number of special freights from Feltham to Brent on the Midland main line. From January to April 1966, when the haulage of the Brighton to Plymouth train reverted from diesel to steam haulage between Brighton and Salisbury, No 73082 was one of 41 steam locomotives used on this service in those months.

Withdrawn from service on 19th June 1966, No 73082 was sold to Woodham Brothers for scrapping at their yard in Barry, where it arrived on 1st November 1966. As is now well documented, the yard concentrated on cutting up withdrawn goods wagons and over 200 locomotives, which had prolonged stays of execution there, were eventually rescued by preservationists. A fund was set up to save the only survivor of the SR's named Standard class 5s. The 73082 Camelot Locomotive Society purchased the engine, without a tender, for £8,100 in January 1979. It left Barry on 24th October 1979 and was moved to the Bluebell Railway where the long and painstaking task of restoring the locomotive to full working order was finally completed in October 1995.

Above left: **No 73082 at Stewarts Lane, its first shed.** Lens of Sutton

Above right: **No 73082 arrives at Dover on 2nd August 1955.** L Hanson

Below: **No 73082 was recorded passing Herne Hill with a morning Victoria to Ramsgate train in June 1956. A 4-SUB electric multiple unit can be seen on the right hand side of the picture.** D W Winkworth

Above: **On a down special which had originated on the WR, No 73082 is seen near Whitstable, on 13th September 1958.** D W Winkworth

Below: **Not long after its overhaul there, the newly named** *Camelot* **was photographed at Eastleigh on 29th August 1959.** R A Panting

Below: **The scene at the Woodham Brothers scrapyard at Barry on Sunday 23rd February 1975: No 73082 is parked next to 'Merchant Navy' class 35022** *Holland America Line* **and 'West Country' class 34101** *Hartland.* **Fortunately, all three of these locomotives survived into preservation. No 73082 left Barry on 24th October 1979.** R L Inns

No 75027

No 75027 was one of the BR Standard class 4 lightweight 4-6-0s designed with a high route availability for secondary main line and cross-country duties. The design work was entrusted to the drawing office at Brighton Works. In many respects the class can be viewed as a tender-engine version of the LM&SR Stanier 2-6-4 tanks. Lot numbers were issued for 90 locomotives, but this was reduced by ten due to the onset of dieselisation. All 80 locomotives in the class were built at Swindon, No 75027 was one of the ten, Nos 75020 to 75029, built to Lot 400.

At Swindon Works, No 75027's frames had been laid and cylinders fitted by 21st March 1954. Its boiler was mounted on the frames by 25th April 1954 and it entered traffic on 17th May 1954. Its original tender was a BR2 type, No 891, though it was subsequently paired with tender numbers 825, 827 and finally 828.

It entered service at Plymouth's Laira Depot in May 1954. After only five months in the West Country, it was transferred to Reading shed in October 1954, then on to Oxford shed in the December of that year. By February 1959 No 75027 was allocated to Swindon, but during the next 14 months it spent some time on loan to Shrewsbury.

In April 1960 it was transferred again, this time to Templecombe, where it was regularly worked on the Somerset & Dorset Joint line. The locomotive moved in November 1962 from Dorset to Wales, first to Machynlleth, to operate on the former Cambrian Railway lines, and then on 9th March 1963 to Croes Newydd shed near Wrexham.

Below: **Not long after it entered service, No 75027 pilots an unidentified 'King' through Totnes at the start of the climb up Rattrey bank, on the down 'Cornish Riviera Express'.** R L Inns collection

Near the end of No 75027's lengthy spell at Oxford, the locomotive powers a fitted goods bound for Morris Cowley, near Knowle & Dorridge station on the former GWR route south of Birmingham, on 8th July 1958. Michael Mensing

Left: **We have two views of the locomotive during its sojourn on the Somerset & Dorset. Here No 75027 is assisting the now also preserved Standard class 5 No 73050 near Midford, on the 10.05 am train from Bournemouth West on 19th August 1961.** D W Winkworth

Below: **Again on the S&D, No 75027 pilots rebuilt 'West Country' Pacific No 34039 *Boscastle*, also now preserved, on the 4.20pm from Bath Green Park at Cole, on 28th July 1962.** D W Winkworth

Croes Newydd passed from Western to London Midland Region control on 9th September 1963, being recoded to 6C from 89B. From that date onwards, until withdrawal, No 75027 remained under LMR jurisdiction.

It is quite remarkable that No 75027 was attached to twelve different depots during its short fourteen year working life. On 31st January 1965 it was transferred to LMR's North Western lines, being allocated to Bank Hall. From 8th November 1965 it spent a year in store at Bank Hall, being kept under cover in serviceable condition. More transfers were to follow, on 8th November 1966 to Skipton, in January 1967 to Carnforth and in April 1967 to Tebay. By May 1967 it was in store at Carlisle Upperby shed. On 27th January 1968 it was observed dumped out of use at Carlisle Kingmoor. This period of inactivity was short-lived, as No 75027 and other members of its class were put to work at Oxenholme banking trains up Grayrigg incline. No 75027 had the dubious distinction of being the last steam locomotive to be used for banking there on 4th May 1968.

Its final regular duty, shared with sister locomotive No 75019, was on the Grassington branch. It worked the 7.25am from Skipton to Swinden Quarry, returning an hour or so later. The train normally conveyed hoppers to Bamber Bridge, but on several occasions was diverted via Appleby. At this time Nos 75019 and 75027 were kept in immaculate condition by enthusiasts. No 75027 was one of five of the class to remain in traffic until the end of steam on 3rd August 1968.

It was stored at Carnforth shed from August to October 1968 from where it was purchased for preservation and delivered to the Bluebell Railway on 22nd January 1969.

Right: **No 75027 at work on the Grassington branch, in the last months of steam operations on BR in 1968. The locomotive still carries the 27A plate of Bank Hall shed which it had left in November 1966.**
G W Sharpe

No 78059

The Derby designed BR Standard class 2 2-6-0 was a versatile and useful type which was almost identical to the LM&SR Ivatt class 2 which continued to be built by BR after nationalisation. The 65 members of the class, numbered 78000 to 78064, all built at Darlington Works, were the only BR standard class not to have the high running plate which distinguished the others .

No 780590 was the fifth of the final batch of 10 locomotives constructed in 1956. In the early stages of construction in July, and almost complete by 12th August, No 78059 entered traffic on 4th September 1956 with BR8 boiler No 1839 and type BR3 tender No 1504. Whilst it is known to have been fitted with replacement boiler No 1841, most likely during a light intermediate overhaul at Crewe in 1960, it appears to have retained the same tender until it was withdrawn.

No 78059 in Holyhead shed yard.
D P Townson, courtesy J Peden

Its first allocation was to Chester Northgate shed, being used on services to Manchester. On 11th April 1959 it was transferred to Llandudno Junction. On 26th April 1964 it was reallocated on loan to Holyhead shed, and transferred again in October 1964 to Bangor. During its time in Wales it was employed on a variety of services including the lighter stopping and semi-fast trains on the North Wales coast line.

When Bangor shed closed on 12th June 1965, No 78059 was transferred to Willesden in London. It was used hauling empty coaching stock and on pilot work at Euston station.

Following Willesden depot's closure to steam on 27th September 1965, No 78059 was reallocated, along with sister locomotives Nos 78018 and 78019 (both now preserved), to Nuneaton. In April 1966 it was in store there with Nos 44866 and 46520. Nuneaton shed closed on 6th June 1966, though No 78059 remained active there for some time after this even though by now it was officially on the books of Stoke shed. In the week ending 10th August 1966 it moved again to its final shed, Crewe South.

Withdrawn from service in November 1966, it remained in store at Crewe South from then until April 1967, when it was sold for scrap to Woodham Brothers. It had arrived at the scrapyard by the end of June 1967. It lingered there for almost 16 years until purchased by the Bluebell Railway, which took delivery of the locomotive on 23rd May 1983. It was the 145th locomotive to leave the Barry scrapyard and became the 30th in the Bluebell Railway's collection.

Given that no Standard class 2s were allocated to Southern Region sheds, No 78059 may seem an odd locomotive for the Bluebell Railway. No example of either of the two classes of BR Standard 2-6-2 tank, both of which worked on the Southern Region at varying times, has been preserved. The smaller of the two types, the 84xxx class, was in fact a tank engine version of the 78xxx class tender locomotives. In November 1965 10 of these tank engines were reallocated to the SR. One of these, No 84014, was sent to Eastleigh to enable the class to be assessed as possible replacements for the elderly O2 0-4-4 tanks in use on the Isle of Wight.

The decision to close most of the island's railways and electrify the remaining line put paid to this idea.

In an imaginative plan to recreate a class lost to preservation, the Bluebell Railway intends to rebuild No 78059 as the fictitiously numbered 84030, the next number in the 84xxx sequence which was never issued by British Railways. In this way, a type lost will be recreated and visitors to the Bluebell Railway in the future will be able to speculate how things might have looked on the Isle of Wight if some of these locomotives had crossed the Solent.

Above: **No 78059 shunting in the yard at Bethesda in 1960. The short branch off the North Wales coast line to Bethesda closed not long after this picture was taken. No 78059 was allocated to Bangor shed at this time.** J S Gilks

Right: **The shape of things to come? No 84029, the last of its class to be built, was also the last steam locomotive to be constructed at Darlington Works. When No 78059 is rebuilt as a tank locomotive, it will take the next number in the 84xxx sequence, becoming No 84030.** E Haigh collection

No 80100

It is most appropriate that an example of the BR Standard class 4 tank has been preserved on the Bluebell Railway, for not only was most of this class built at Brighton, but they were used on the Bluebell line before BR abandoned it.

No 80100 was built at Brighton Works to Order No BR6167 which authorised the construction of 17 locomotives, Nos 80089 to 80105. It left Brighton Works on 31st January 1955 and was officially allocated to Plaistow shed from that date. However Brighton shed made use of it during February 1955 on at least two occasions as a substitute for failed Bulleid Pacifics. Subsequently it took up duties at Plaistow shed in east London, working on the former London, Tilbury & Southend Railway's busy commuter services between Fenchurch Street station in London, Southend and Shoeburyness. It was transferred to Tilbury on 31st October 1959 just before Plaistow shed closed on 2nd November.

During its time working on the former LT&SR routes, it received two non-classified repairs at Bow Works, two repairs at Stratford Works in East London, and two general overhauls at Darlington, the latter in 1958 and 1961.

Initially the Standard class 4 tanks had been allocated to all regions of BR except the Western, however the WR became host to many of these engines which were made redundant when the lines from Fenchurch Street were electrified. No 80100 was one of these, transferred initially to Stratford in June 1962, on 15th July it passed from Eastern to Western Region stock. During the next four weeks it was transferred to its final shed, Shrewsbury.

Regional boundary changes on 1st January 1963 meant that Shrewsbury passed from Western to London Midland Region control, the depot being recoded from 89A to 6D. At Shrewsbury No 80100 was used on local stopping passenger services in the area, including those on the now preserved Severn Valley line to Bridgnorth and Kidderminster. During this time it was also seen at Aberystwyth and Whitchurch and on Hereford to Gloucester trains.

No 80100 was withdrawn from service in the latter part of 1965 and put into store at Shrewsbury. Sold to Woodham's at Barry, in December 1965, it in fact already had arrived in the lower Docks area at Barry by 1st November 1965.

Purchased for preservation by the Bluebell Railway at a cost of £7,500 in October 1977, No 80100 in company with No 30847 arrived at Sheffield Park on 11th October 1978.

Below: **On its third day in traffic, the brand new No 80100 is in immaculate condition at Brighton shed on 2nd February 1955.** R L Inns collection

Bottom: **Substituting for a Bulleid Pacific on a train for the lines west of Brighton, No 80100 waits for the right of way at Brighton station on 2nd February 1955.** R L Inns collection

Right: **Bereft of its smokebox number plate and without a shed plate, No 80100 is pictured at Shrewsbury in early 1963.**
R L Inns collection

Below: **In a scene which in theory at least could be recreated today No 80100 pauses at Bridgnorth station on the Severn Valley line whilst hauling the 1.45pm Shrewsbury to Bewdley service on 6th July 1963, not long before the route lost its passenger services.** John Edgington

No 92240

The 9F class 2-10-0 was arguably the best of the BR standard designs. Intended as freight-only engines, the class will however be remembered more as mixed-traffic locomotives.

A total of 251 9Fs were put into service. No 92240 was one of 198 constructed at Crewe Works, the remaining 53 were built at Swindon. Building commenced in 1954 and was completed in March 1960 when No 92220 *Evening Star*, the last steam locomotive built for BR, was turned out from Swindon Works.

No 92240 was built at Crewe, to Swindon Lot No 433 and Crewe Works Order No E497, which was for 30 locomotives, Nos 92221 to 92250. The average cost of building this batch was £30,200. The cost of No 92240's boiler alone came to £6,415.

No 92240 entered traffic on 1st October 1958, fitted with BR9 boiler No 1931, equipped with a double chimney and type BR1G tender, No 1551. Its first allocation was to Ebbw Junction shed at Newport in South Wales. There it was used on heavy coal and iron ore trains. From 19th to 21st November 1958 it was in Swindon Works for an unclassified repair, during which time ATC equipment was fitted. On emerging from the works it was transferred to Old Oak Common shed in London, where it was used on a variety of freights on the former GWR lines to the west and to Birmingham. The Industrial Holiday fortnight in Birmingham in August 1959 saw the use of 9F 2-10-0s on passenger trains from Snow Hill Station, Nos 92240 and 92244 being observed on trains to the south.

In September 1960 No 92240 was transferred down the GWR main line from Old Oak Common to Southall. It entered Eastleigh Works in July 1964 for an overhaul, following which on 12th and 26th September 1964 it was observed at Eastleigh shed.

No 92240 was placed in store in July 1965 and was withdrawn from service in the following month, after less than seven years service. It was sold to Woodham Brothers for scrap and had arrived at Barry by 2nd February 1966.

The 9F was purchased by the Bluebell Railway for preservation, at a cost of £10,500, though this did not include a tender. Transportation from Barry cost a further £2,700. It was the 93rd locomotive and the first 9F to leave Woodham's yard, departing on 5th October 1978, arriving the following day at Sheffield Park.

Painted in unlined black and in relatively clean condition. No 92240 reposes in the yard of its home shed at Southall on 15th September 1962. No 92240 underwent a heavy intermediate overhaul at Swindon works which took from 17th November 1961 to 2nd March 1962 to complete. Sister locomotive No 92233 had a similar overhaul there at the same period. It appears that No 92233 emerged from the works with the tender from No 92240, while No 92240 got the BR1G tender No 1544 from No 92233. No 92240 is seen here with the tender received in the Swindon exchange.
A Linaker, courtesy Mike Esau

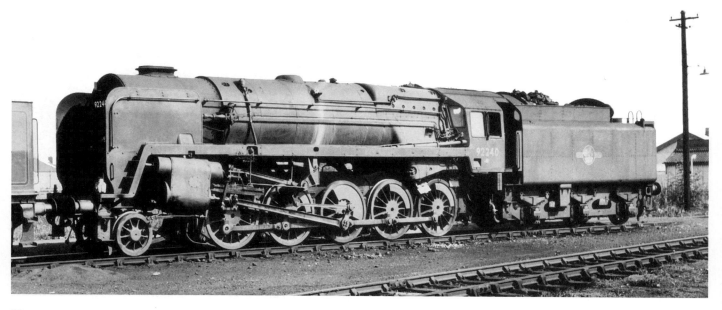

Right: **No 92240 hauls an up freight through at West Drayton & Yiewsley Station on 19th October 1963.** Brian Stephenson

Below: **Another view of No 92240 at Southall shed in 1963.** R L Inns collection

No 4 *Sharpthorn*

The present Bluebell Railway was part of the line from Culver Junction (formerly Barcombe Junction) to East Grinstead Low Level, which was built by the Lewes & East Grinstead Railway. The Act of Parliament authorising its construction was passed in 1877 and it was formally opened on 1st August 1882. It was acquired by the London, Brighton & South Coast Railway under powers granted in 1878.

Sharpthorn has an early link with the Bluebell Railway because it was used in the construction of the line. The locomotive is an example of the Manning Wardle company's standard type of 0-6-0 saddle tank engine designed for industrial users. It was built at the company's Boyne Engine Works, in Leeds, in 1877, and allocated their works number, 641.

The locomotive was eventually acquired by Samuel Williams & Sons Limited, Contractors, of Dagenham in Essex, becoming No 4 in their fleet. In 1903 it was withdrawn from service and put into store. During a period of engine shortages in 1909 it was brought out again and refurbished, to see nearly another 50 years of service. The locomotive's present boiler dates from 1934.

By 1958 it was still being maintained in excellent condition. Its livery, and that of another locomotive at Samuel Williams' works, was sky blue. The firm owned eight engines in total. The other six were turned out in a red livery similar to that of the old Midland Railway, lined out in black and yellow. By the late 1950s the Company was keen to have the locomotive preserved, if somewhere could be found to keep it, preferably in the south of England. Unfortunately there were no takers so it was preserved by the firm at its works in Dagenham.

In order for it to be present at events marking the centenary of the opening of the Lewes & East Grinstead Railway, *Sharpthorn* was loaned to the Bluebell, arriving there on 3rd April 1982. Unfortunately Samuel Williams & Sons Limited went into liquidation while it was there. The company's receivers subsequently sold *Sharpthorn* for £1,500 to the Bluebell Railway, the transaction being completed by May 1984.

No 4 at the Dagenham yard of Samuel Williams & Sons Limited, probably in 1958.
J Peden

Blue Circle

This geared 2-2-0 tank, works number 9449, was built in 1926 by Aveling & Porter Limited at Rochester in Kent. This company, best known for road vehicles, had adapted their design of road haulage traction engine for use on rails. Two basic types for rail use were built. One had four wheels of equal size coupled by means of spur gearing or chains. The other pattern, of which this locomotive is an example, could best be described as a 2-2-0. The rear wheels which took the drive were considerably larger than the leading wheels.

Mr William Lee Roberts, the last Managing Director of William Lee, Son & Company Ltd, founded the Holborough Cement Company in about 1923. Although this type of locomotive was quite obsolete by 1926, Mr Roberts had grown up with locomotives of this design at Lee's works and it is said that out of sentiment the first locomotive he ordered for the Holborough works was of an identical type.

It was sold new to the Holborough Cement Company Limited for shunting duties at its works at Snodland in Kent. The locomotive was delivered on 4th February 1926. This company was taken over by the Associated Portland Cement Manufacturers Limited in 1931. The locomotive spent its entire working life there and remained in fairly constant use until about 1960. Thereafter it was used as a standby and was steamed only occasionally.

In 1964 the Associated Portland Cement Company presented the locomotive to the Bluebell Railway and it was delivered there on 23rd April 1964. It was given the name 'Blue Circle', a trademark of the donating company.

The traction engine ancestry of the locomotive is apparent in this view taken on 7th July 1956. D W Winkworth

No 3 *Baxter*

Fletcher Jennings & Company Limited specialised in the construction of more than 12 designs of small tank engine, in both standard and narrow gauges, for sale to industry.

This 0-4-0T (works No 158 of 1877), was built to Fletcher Jennings' class B design, at their Lowca Works at Whitehaven, in what is now Cumbria, for the Dorking Greystone Lime Company Limited. It was originally obtained from Fletcher Jennings on a hire purchase agreement, at a cost of £1,020.

It was used by the Dorking Greystone Lime Company on the standard gauge lines in the quarry at Betchworth from 1877 until the Company ceased trading in 1959. The Company also had a 3ft 2¼in gauge system at the quarry, which was operated by two Fletcher Jennings 0-4-0 tanks, Nos 4 *Townsend Hook* and 5 *William Finlay*, both named after directors.

When the quarry closed both locomotives were stored and exhibited at Sheffield Park on the Bluebell Railway, before moving to their respective preservation sites at Brockham Museum and a private collection at Woking.

No 3 *Baxter* was delivered to the Bluebell Railway on 15th August 1960 and was the third locomotive in the railway's collection. It was originally placed on loan by the late Major E W Taylorson of the Dorking Greystone Lime Company Limited. Major Taylorson's executors later agreed to allow the engine to remain there.

Top: **Shortly after 1932 the locomotive was repainted and lined out, and the name *Captain Baxter* and the number 3 were inscribed on the tank sides. Captain Baxter was one of the founder directors of the Dorking Greystone Lime Company Limited. Some evidence of the painted name and number appear on this photograph, taken at the Eastern Battery on 26th August 1950. The metal nameplates *Baxter* and numberplates were applied in 1947.** D W Winkworth

Below: ***Baxter* at Betchworth circa 1953, out of steam, probably during a weekend. Also working in the quarry was a vertical boiler**

0-4-0 locomotive nicknamed 'Coffeepot', built by Thomas Howard Head and now preserved at Beamish Museum. J Peden

No 1972 *Stamford*

This 0-6-0 saddle tank was built for industrial use by the Avonside Engine Company Bristol, with works No 1972, in 1927. It was sold new to the Staveley Coal & Iron Company for use in their ironstone quarry at Pilton in Rutland. There it was used to haul wagons to the exchange sidings by the main line.

The quarry was subsequently taken over by Stewart & Lloyds Minerals Limited. *Stamford* was allotted their fleet number 8310/24 and continued to be used into the late 1960s. When Stewart & Lloyds reduced their rail operations, No 24, along with some other engines, became redundant.

At the time, the Bluebell Railway had a fleet of only eight locomotives capable of hauling passenger trains and was looking for extra power.

Stamford was purchased with this in mind, and was delivered to the Bluebell Railway on 25th October 1969.

Below: *Stamford* **in use in the quarry at Pilton on 21st May 1966.** John Edgington

No 957 *Britannia*

This 4-wheeled petrol-driven locomotive was built in 1926 at the agricultural engineering works of J & F Howard Limited, as works No 957, for their own internal use. It has a 25hp engine and is capable of a top speed of 8mph. The first serious attempts to apply the internal combustion engine to railway use were made during the course of the First World War and this is a late example of that first generation, which were generally petrol-engined.

This picture of *Britannia* was taken at Sheffield Park on 6th December 1970.
R L Inns

In 1932 Howard's works at Bedford were taken over by the Britannia Iron & Steel Works Limited, who were responsible for the naming of the locomotive. Some time after 1951 the unofficial number 70000 was painted on the back of the cab, this number of course being the same as the BR Standard class 7 prototype, built in 1951.

Britannia was replaced by a more powerful locomotive in 1965 and its owners donated No 957 to the Bluebell Railway Preservation Society. It was delivered to Sheffield Park on 8th March 1965.

This is the only non steam locomotive on the Bluebell Railway. It is also a source of frustration to the authors. The aim of this book has been to present pictures of the locomotives in the Bluebell fleet, as they were, before preservation. We regret to report that we have failed to fully achieve our objectives, with a double dose of irony, on this, the very last page of the book, for pictures of this locomotive, the only internal combustion engine machine on the railway, before it went to the Bluebell have completely eluded us. Perhaps someone, might have a suitable picture which could be incorporated into a future edition of this book?